Famous and Fabulous Journeys

Famous and Fabulous
Journeys

text by Bernard Barbuk   illustrations by Frank Baber

Peter ⚜ Lowe

The translation of "The Greenlanders' Saga"
which appears on p. 10 is reproduced from
Westward to Vinland by Helge Ingstad, by kind
permission of the publishers, Jonathan Cape.

The following writers have contributed to
this book:
Teresa Armstrong pp. 66, 90
Carol Berkson p. 18
Lucy Berman pp. 50, 102
Peter Brent p. 58
Bruce Leigh pp. 30, 98, 106
John Milsome pp. 46, 62, 78, 86, 94, 110

Casebound edition with jacket
ISBN 0 85654 015 3

Casebound edition with picture boards
ISBN 0 85654 016 1

Printed in Belgium by Henri Proost & Co. Turnhout

List of Stories

Introduction

The longing to make journeys, to go travelling, is one of the primary instincts of man, and a mark of his essential curiosity. For even though in the earliest times it was the need to find fresh supplies of food that usually sent men wandering, it seems that there have always been people who would climb hills just to see what lay on the other side, cross deep rivers just to walk where no-one had walked before, or wander in forests just for the joy of exploring.

Not surprisingly, the people who went on these journeys—especially the ones who came back—were often credited with supernatural powers, and their stories became involved with religion and superstition. One such example is the story of Odysseus' wanderings, which you will find in this book.

Today, when travelling is a commonplace, comfortable, high-speed affair, the appeal of the other, dangerous, type of journey is as strong as ever. Men climbed Mount Everest "because it was there". Men travelled to the moon not primarily for profit or conquest, but because space is the next frontier of human knowledge. Men and women sail around the world singlehanded, or in tiny boats, or cross vast distances of difficult terrain, for the sheer pleasure of doing so, of proving that it is possible. And everyone is fascinated by their achievements!

This book contains examples of many kinds of journeys. Some were triumphs of skill and daring; some succeeded by strokes of luck. Some ended badly, many threatened to. All have one thing in common—adventure. It is this common theme that makes stories about journeys, whether fact or fiction, some of the best stories of all.

Bernard Barbuk

A voyage to Vinland

Towards the end of the ninth century, a great Viking expedition set out from Iceland to settle in the strange, new country of Greenland. It was led by a Norwegian named Eirik the Red. With around five hundred people, with animals, food and weapons, he founded a settlement which was to be the first stepping stone to the New World.

The Vikings were probably the greatest sea-faring people there have ever been. Coming from Norway, Sweden and Denmark, they depended on the sea for most of their food and they soon learned to make use of the knowledge they were forced to acquire to stay alive.

At first their expeditions were small—raiding parties racing across the North Sea to the coasts of England and Scotland, and scurrying back with their spoils. Gradually they became more ambitious and during their great age, which began about 800 A.D. they travelled far and wide in their fine, swift ships: across the Baltic Sea to Russia, south to Scotland, England, Normandy and the Mediterranean, west to Ireland, Iceland and Greenland.

Though they were ferocious raiders, the Vikings were also interested in exploration and discovery. Their own lands were harsh and they were always looking for places to found new settlements. The remains of Viking houses and farms have been found in many places in Europe and in Scotland and north-eastern England traces of their language remain even now in the names of towns and villages.

By the middle of the ninth century, Vikings were well established in Iceland. For such an adventurous race it was only natural to sail still further west across the Atlantic. Eirik the Red's "colony" in Greenland was, according to legend, the starting point for a new voyage of discovery which was to lead them to a land they called Vinland and which we know as North America.

The story of this great journey comes from two Icelandic *Sagas*, tales of the adventures of the Vikings which were written down towards the end of the fourteenth century. The extract here is from *The Green-*

landers' Saga. It tells how a man called Bjarni Herjolfsson set out from Iceland to spend the winter with his father at the Greenland settlement. He had not made the journey before and on the way he was blown off course and later got lost in a fog. He saw three new and strange lands but as they did not fit the descriptions he had heard of Greenland, he passed by and eventually arrived safely at his father's house. Some time later Eirik the Red's son, Leif Eiriksson, decided to find out more about the mysterious lands to the west.

The account of the journey seems very matter-of-fact but it is important to remember as you read it that the Vikings had no compasses, no engines, only their sails and oars; and that the cold seas they crossed are among the most hazardous in the world.

There was now much talk of voyages of exploration. Leif, the son of Eirik the Red of Brattahlid, came to see Bjarni Herjolfsson and purchased his ship and engaged a crew —they were thirty-five men in all.

Leif asked his father Eirik to lead the expedition. Eirik tried to excuse himself, pointing out that he was too old now and did not have the strength to endure all hardships as he had done before. Leif maintained that he was the one in their family who commanded the most luck as a leader. Eirik then gave in to Leif, and as soon as they were ready they rode off to the ships. But when only a short distance away from the houses, Eirik's horse stumbled, and he fell off and hurt his foot. Then Eirik said: "It is not my fate to discover any more lands than the one in which we now live. We shall not travel together any farther." Eirik returned home to Brattahlid, but Leif went on board the ship with thirty-five men. Among them was a Southerner, whose name was Tyrkir.

Now they prepared their ship and put out to sea as soon as they were ready, and they found first the land which Bjarni had seen last. They sailed in to the shore, cast anchor, lowered a boat, and went ashore, but they did not see any grass there. The uplands consisted of huge glaciers, and between the glaciers and the shore the land was just like one single slab or rock. The land seemed to be of no value.

Then Leif said: "At least it has not happened to us what happened to Bjarni in this land, that we did not go ashore. Now I will give this land a name, it should be called Helluland (Flat Stone Land)." They then returned to their ship.

They put out to sea and found the second land. This time too they sailed in to the coast and cast anchor, lowered a boat and went ashore. The country was flat and covered with forests, and wherever they went there were white sandy beaches sloping gently down to the sea. Then Leif said: "We shall give this land a name according to its natural resources, and call it Markland (Forest Land)." After that they hurried back to their ship.

They then sailed out to sea before a north-east wind and were at sea two days before sighting land. They sailed in towards it and came to an island which lay north of the mainland. There they went ashore and looked around, and the weather was fine. They saw that there was dew on the grass, and it came about that they got some of it on their hands and put it to their lips, and they thought that they had never before tasted anything so sweet.

They then returned to their ship and sailed into the sound which lay between the island and the cape projecting northward from the mainland. They sailed westward past the cape. It was very shallow there at low tide. Their ship went aground, and it was a long way from the ship to shore. But they were so impatient to get to land that they did not want to wait for the tide to rise under their ship but ran ashore at a place where a river flowed out of a lake.

As soon as the tide had refloated the ship

they took their boat and rowed out to it, and brought the ship farther up the river and into the lake. There they cast anchor and carried their leather bags ashore and put up their booths. They later decided to winter there, and built large houses.

There was no lack of salmon in the river or in the lake, and they were bigger salmon than they had ever seen before. The land was so bountiful that it seemed to them that the cattle would not need fodder during the winter. There was no frost in winter, and the grass hardly withered. Day and night were of more equal length than in Greenland and Iceland. On the shortest day of the year the sun was visible in the middle of the afternoon as well as at breakfast time.

When they had finished building their houses, Leif said to his men: "I now intend to divide our party into two groups and explore the country. One group is to stay here at the houses, the other is to get to know the country, but not to go so far away that they are not able to get back home in the evening, and they are not to be separated from each other."

This they did for a time, and Leif took turns, at one time going off with those who explored the land, at other times staying by the houses.

Leif was a big and strong man, and very impressive in appearance. He was shrewd and clever, temperate, and highly respected in every way.

It happened one evening that one man was missing, and it was Tyrkir, the Southerner. Leif was much distressed by this, for Tyrkir had been with his father for a long time and he had been very fond of Leif when he was a child. Leif spoke harsh words to his companions and prepared to look for him and took twelve men with him. But when they had gone only a short distance away from the camp Tyrkir came walking towards them. They were very happy to see him. Leif could see at once that Tyrkir's spirits were high.

Tyrkir had a bulging forehead and a small freckled face with roving eyes: he was a small and insignificant man but was handy at all sorts of crafts.

Leif said to him: "Why are you so late, foster-father, and why did you not stay in the company of the others?" Tyrkir at first spoke a long time in German, rolling his eyes and grimacing, but the others did not understand what he was saying. A little later he said in the Norse tongue: "I did not walk much farther than you, but I can report on something new: I have found vines and grapes."

"Is that true, foster-father?" Leif said.

"It is certainly true," Tyrkir replied, "for I was born where there is no lack of vines and grapes."

They slept there that night, but in the morning Leif said to his crew: "From now on we shall have two tasks to do and we shall alternate them so as to do each job every other day. We shall gather grapes and we shall cut vines and fell timber, to make a cargo for my ship." This was done. It is said that their pinnace was filled with grapes.

A full cargo was cut for the ship, and in the spring they made ready and sailed away. Leif gave the country a name in accordance with its resources, and called it Vinland (Wineland).

Scholars have argued for many years about how much of this story is true and about the exact area that the Vikings discovered. Many thought that it must be in the south of North America, where wild grapes grow, but no Viking remains have ever been found there. In 1960 a Norwegian archaeologist, Helge Ingstad, following the descriptions and distances given in the *Sagas*, found the first traces of a real Viking settlement in Newfoundland. There now seems little doubt that, five hundred years before Columbus, the Vikings journeyed to Vinland and discovered the North American continent for the first time.

The return of Odysseus

The two most famous Greek traditional stories are the *Iliad* and the *Odyssey*. The *Iliad* tells the story of the siege of Troy, when the armies of Greece fought to rescue Helen from the Trojans. The *Odyssey*, on which this story is based, tells what happened to the Greek hero Odysseus after the great war was over, and why the short journey from Troy to his home took him ten long years.

The author of both epics is known as Homer but in fact they were probably written down by different people at different times somewhere between 500 and 1000BC. Before they were written down they were passed on by professional storytellers who knew the stories by heart and, no doubt, changed them here and there each time they told them. Both the *Iliad* and the *Odyssey* contain a mixture of invention and real happenings. Many of the characters (the Cyclops, for example) are not just fantastic monsters, but symbolize beliefs or customs.

Because the original is so long, some exciting adventures have had to be left out. If you want to read more about Odysseus and his companions there are many good translations both in prose and in verse.

The battle was over. The young men who had plotted to seize the throne of Ithaca while Odysseus was away lay dead for Odysseus was home at last. It was nineteen years since he had left his island kingdom of Ithaca to fight in the great siege of Troy and no one had heard from him for ten years. Only Penelope his wife believed he was still alive and steadfastly refused to marry any of the ambitious young men who told her every day that he would never return. What had happened to Odysseus in those ten years? And what had happened to the twelve long-prowed ships and the hundreds of well-armed men with whom he began his journey?

The first serious trouble had come to Odysseus and his men when they arrived at the land of the Cyclops. The Cyclops were a barbarous race of giants with one eye each set in the middle of their foreheads. Once they had been skilled in metalwork, but now they kept large flocks of sheep and goats. Though they lived like shepherds, keeping their animals and living with them in large caves, they still thought themselves at least the equals of the immortal gods.

Odysseus could not restrain his curiosity about the Cyclops but, realizing the dangers, he acted cautiously. He left most of his men behind and picked only twelve companions

15

to go with him to reconnoitre. At first all went well. They found a great area of animal pens and then an enormous cave. When Odysseus' men went in they found it was empty except for large stores of cheeses and milk, though it was obvious that many animals lived there.

This was the cave of a Cyclops called Polyphemus. Odysseus's men wanted simply to take as much cheese as they could carry but Odysseus himself was determined to wait and meet the giant. He soon got his wish. As evening came, Polyphemus returned home, driving his flocks of fat sheep and silky-coated goats in front of him into the cave. Then, unfortunately, he did something Odysseus had not bargained for: he closed the cave entrance after him with an enormous boulder, far too heavy for Odysseus and his men to shift. Whatever happened next, Odysseus and his men realized they could only leave the cave if Polyphemus moved the stone for them.

If Odysseus had hoped for a friendly reception from Polyphemus he was sadly disillusioned. As soon as the Cyclops saw the little group of Greeks he seized two of them in one enormous hand, dashed their heads on the cave floor and gulped them down with one swallow.

Odysseus and his men were trapped, doomed it seemed to be eaten by the horrible creature. Vengeance now became Odysseus' one aim. His problem was how to achieve this while keeping Polyphemus sufficiently active to unblock the cave entrance. While Polyphemus lay snoring Odysseus made a crude wooden spear from wood he found in the cave. The next evening when Polyphemus was asleep again, digesting more of Odysseus' companions, a daring plan was carried out. First Odysseus heated the spear point in the fire until it glowed red hot. Then with the help of four of his men the Cyclops' enormous single eyelid was pulled open and Odysseus thrust the sharp burning wood deep into the eye. Polyphemus awoke roar-

ing in agony, clutching at his blinded eye.

The problem of the boulder remained and the Greeks spent an anxious night wondering if they were after all to die in the dark cave. Fortunately for them, even though by morning the Cyclops was exhausted with pain, he heaved the great rock aside as he always did to let his flocks out to pasture. As the animals left the cave, Odysseus and his remaining men were able to escape.

After more adventures they came eventually to the island of Aeaea which was ruled over by the goddess Circe, famous for her skill in magic. This time Odysseus was determined not to take any chances and he sent half his men, well armed, to investigate. Strength and weapons meant nothing to a goddess, of course. Circe received the men politely but during the evening she drugged their food, turned them into grunting pigs and locked them in a sty.

Now the Greeks believed that the gods liked to take an active part in the affairs of mortals from time to time, sometimes even taking on human form themselves. The gods were following Odysseus' voyage with interest, some taking his side, some trying their best to destroy him. Seeing his troubles with Circe, the god Hermes came to Odysseus and gave him some of a sacred plant called Moly which protected him against all her enchantments. With the help of this plant Odysseus was able to force Circe to release his men from her spell. In fact Circe so softened towards them that she let them stay a whole year on her island in the greatest luxury. And though she was not at all pleased when Odysseus asked permission to leave, she gave him all the advice she could about the many dangers that faced him. As you will see, Odysseus had need of this.

The way ahead took the ship past the three greatest hazards Odysseus had to face during the whole long journey. The first danger came when they reached the place where the Sirens sang their deadly songs.

The Sirens were witches, with the faces of beautiful women, but the bodies of birds. Their singing was so sweet that anyone who heard it felt he must get as close as possible to them, only to be dashed to death on the rocky coast where they lived. Warned by Circe, Odysseus blocked the crew's ears with wax. Lashed firmly to the mast, he listened to the beautiful song, the only mortal to hear it and survive.

Though they had been through bad things, still worse were to come. In front of the ship's prow the sea now narrowed between rocky headlands into a single channel, then divided again into two. Odysseus knew that one way led to certain death against the windswept cliffs of the wandering rocks and that the other way was only slightly less dangerous.

"Great Goddess Athene," he murmured, "help me. Which way shall we steer?" He made his choice and the ship sailed on. To his relief he saw in the distance two mighty pinnacles of rock and knew he had chosen right. If they could steer a course between the lairs of the dreadful Scylla and Charybdis, the way ahead would be clear. As they approached, the look-out at the masthead spotted a cave high up on the smooth polished flank of the larger of the two rock masses. From it leered the most horrible creature Odysseus had ever seen, waking or sleeping. It had six heads and six mouths with three rows of teeth in each mouth. Once this awful creature had been a beautiful woman but now she looked more like a dog: twelve dog-like legs hung out of the cave mouth.

"Steer clear, steer clear" cried Odysseus' men in terror. Odysseus, however, kept calm.

"Steer close to her," he ordered. "Steer as far as possible from the other rock."

Circe had told him that while Scylla could only snatch and eat six sailors, the hideous witch Charybdis who sat watching them from under a high fig tree on the other rock could kill them all. Three times each day Charybdis would suck up large quantities of sea and spit it out again, swallowing anything she could eat. Even while Odysseus was urging the men to avoid Charybdis, Scylla leaned over and licked six men off the deck, one with each tongue, for her meal.

They sailed on gloomily until they came to the island of Sicily, the land of the sun god Hyperion, where his seven herds of fat cattle grazed among sun-washed pastures bright with flowers. Despite the peaceful appearance there was danger here. Odysseus had been advised to avoid the island completely, but his men threatened to mutiny unless they had fresh food and water and Odysseus was forced to give in.

"All right," he told the men. "Beach the ship and we'll rest here. But do not touch any of Hyperion's cattle; I warn you—our lives depend on it."

This last command was easier given than obeyed by mere mortals. Contrary winds kept them all on the island for thirty days. Their provisions ran out and they found it impossible to catch enough game to live on. As a result, while Odysseus was asleep one afternoon his men began to slaughter Hyperion's cattle.

Only Odysseus knew exactly how disastrous this deed would prove to be and he began what was to be the final stage of his journey with a sense of impending doom. Sure enough, scarcely had the island sunk out of sight behind the ship when a terrible thunderstorm hit them. Almost immediately the ship was dismasted by a thunderbolt and in seconds another one smashed the long curved ship as if she were a child's toy. The brave crew were crushed and drowned: only Odysseus survived. He lived through another encounter with Charybdis and at long last returned to Ithaca to rescue his patient wife Penelope from the young men who coveted his throne. The story of his long journey home has become one of the best known legends in the world.

Friar William and the Mongols

Towards the middle of the thirteenth century, in the court of King Louis IX in Paris, there was a Franciscan friar named William of Rubruik. Flemish by birth, Friar William had spent many years in Paris, and had become a favourite of the King's.

One afternoon the King sent for him.

"I want you to make a journey for me," he said. "It will be very hazardous, but I know I can rely on you. I have heard that among the Mongol tribes of Asia, there is a chief named Sartach who is a Christian. I want you to go to him and ask him if you can stay and preach Christianity there."

At the King's words, Friar William felt both excitement and fear. Few Europeans had dared to venture to Asia. The land had been overrun by the Mongol tribes—a strange barbarian race who had come from somewhere in China, sweeping across the

land, destroying all that they saw. Little was known of the Mongols except that they were warlike. But if one of their chiefs was a Christian then perhaps there was some hope of turning the Mongols towards peace.

"I will go," said Friar William.

The first part of the journey took the Friar and his companions across Europe to Constantinople, a port on the Black Sea. To them it was the very edge of civilization.

From Constantinople Friar William sailed with a party of four, another friar, two servants and a Russian slave boy. Late in May, in 1253, they landed on Russian soil at the borders of the Mongol empire.

Gathering their few possessions, they set out on horseback. One day passed, then another, with no sign of any man. They rode past towns that had been destroyed by the Mongols. They rode past heaps of bones that lay bleaching in the sun. On the third day, a cloud of dust rose from the plain and they saw a troop of Mongols galloping towards them. Friar William and his party were frightened but they stood their ground. Minutes later they found themselves surrounded.

How strange these Mongol warriors looked to them with their long desert robes and flowing head-dresses. Their faces had a yellowish cast for that was the colour of their race, and their eyes were slanted. Some carried swords; some carried bows and arrows. Friar William felt he had wandered into another world.

"Where are you coming from and where are you going?" they asked.

"We have come from the court of King Louis IX in Paris," the Friar said. "We have heard that there is among you a chief named Sartach who is a Christian. Will you take us to him?"

"No," the headman said. "We will not travel so far. But we will take you to see a chief named Scatay."

Through the night the Friar and his party rode with the Mongol troop, reaching Scatay's camp as the sun rose. It was not a camp on the ground, but a camp on wheels: there were hundreds of carts, each drawn by a team of oxen, each carrying a tent which served as a dwelling place. Friar William was amazed as he watched the carts coming towards him. Here more than ever he felt the strangeness of this land where men had no fixed homes but carried their houses with them, never knowing where they would stop from one night to the next.

They rode with the "camp" all day and when the Mongols stopped in the evening, Friar William was taken to Scatay's tent. The tent frame was a circle of interlaced sticks with a little round hoop at the top to serve as a chimney. The cloth that was thrown over the frame was made of black felt. Near the top and over the entrance there were extra pieces of felt, embroidered with brightly coloured trees, birds, beasts and vines. Inside, Scatay sat on his couch with men and women of his camp on cushions on the floor around him. Like the others, Friar William sat on the floor.

Friar William offered Scatay biscuits and wine, apologizing because his gifts were so humble. Scatay offered the Friar mares' milk to drink—a strange drink to a European's taste, which Friar William drank to show the Mongols his willingness to accept their customs.

"What is your business here?" asked Scatay. Again Friar William expressed his wish to see Sartach and Scatay agreed to provide him with carts and a guide.

The journey was long and hard. It was summer, and most of the land they crossed was desert. Sometimes for days they saw nothing but earth and sky. Always the heat of the sun lay heavy and intense upon them. The Mongols they travelled with were not kind to them. Those they met on the way refused to help them, for Mongols would only give aid in exchange for gifts, and Friar William had nothing left to give them.

Sartach's camp was even larger and more

impressive than Scatay's. After a night's rest Friar William prepared to put his case. He dressed in his priestly robes and gathered his holy objects. Then, chanting a Christian hymn, he entered Sartach's tent.

Sartach watched and listened—but said nothing. He seemed to be more interested in the holy objects than in what Friar William was saying and when the Friar asked if he might stay and preach he did not reply, but simply dismissed him.

All the next day the Friar waited for a word from Sartach and when at last a messenger came the message was not encouraging. First, Friar William must not call Sartach a Christian: he was a Mongol. Second, if he wanted to stay among the Mongols to preach, he must travel still further and ask permission from Batu, Sartach's father.

The next day the party set out once more and a few days later reached Batu's camp. Soon Friar William was called to Batu's tent. So powerful was the presence of this great warrior chief that for a moment Friar William felt it was God he knelt to. Rising, he made his request once more and once more the chief listened in silence and then dismissed him.

Batu was not as quick to answer as Sartach had been. For five weeks Friar William waited for an answer. Though all this time he and his party travelled with Batu's men, they were given neither carts nor horses. They had to travel on foot, they were given little food and had only the ground to rest on. Somehow they managed to keep their spirits up, and each day Friar William was able to record the details of the journey.

Finally an aid of Batu's came to see them. Batu had decided to send him to Mangu Khan, chief of all the Mongols, there to make yet again his request to stay and preach among them. The journey, Friar William was told, would take four months, through weather so cold that stones and trees split right in two with the frost.

This time the Europeans were given sheepskin gowns, breeches, boots, hoods and felt stockings. They were also provided with horses to ride.

Each day they travelled as far as they could, without stopping. Often Friar William and the rest were hungry and thirsty and always, it seemed, they were tired and cold. When they stopped to make camp at night it was after dark and often they could find no fuel to make a fire. They were given raw meat to eat and slept huddled together in the cold and darkness. At last, two days after Christmas in 1253 they arrived at Mangu's camp.

A week later Friar William dressed once again in his priestly robes, and stood on Mangu's threshold. The scene inside was a splendid one. The walls of the tent were made of cloth of gold. Mangu sat on a couch surrounded by his courtiers and his women, a dung fire blazing before him. After the cold and hardships the Friar had suffered, this was luxury indeed.

Like the other chiefs before him, however, Mangu Khan turned down the Friar's request, but at least he gave him leave to stay till the winter ended. For two months Friar William stayed with Mangu's camp, trying to preach his faith to the Mongols. Every day he moved among them and spoke to them, but no-one would listen.

Spring came. Mangu Khan sent for the Friar, explaining that he could stay no longer, he must return to Europe. The Mongols, he said, had their own god to pray to; they did not trust him or his Christian god.

Friar William's sad return journey took over a year, but by 1255 he was back in Paris again. His mission to convert the Mongols had been a failure, but the record of his journey was to be of great value to later travellers, telling them something of the Mongols, their customs and their strange land.

Westward to a new world

The world of the middle and late fifteenth century was hungry for two things: spices and gold. Spices were used to bring variety to the limited choice of food available even to the rich. Gold, as a universal currency, was necessary to finance the trade in spices and the general expansion of trade and industry which was going on at that time.

Though the spice trade was fabulously wealthy, the wealth was not easily won. Spices such as nutmeg, cinnamon and pepper had to be brought all the way from the Far East and as most of the trip was overland, the journey could take several years.

Moreover the terminus for this trade was the countries of the eastern Mediterranean —the Levant as it was called—and here the Venetians and to some extent the Genoese had a virtual monopoly and charged very high prices.

As ship-building and the science of navigation improved, men's thoughts naturally began to turn to the task of finding the sea route to the "Indies"—India, Java, the Moluccas—where the valuable spices grew.

"Wherever ship has sailed, there have I journeyed." So wrote Christobal Colon, whom we call Christopher Columbus, shortly before setting out on a journey which was to change not only man's understanding of geography, but the history of the world.

Columbus was, technically, an Italian, for

he was born near Genoa in 1446 or 1451. However, he may have been of Spanish descent, for he spoke and wrote exclusively in Spanish.

He went to sea while he was still only fourteen, but he was by no means uneducated, and had the constant advice of his more learned brother Batholomew (Bartolemeo), a celebrated maker of charts and maps. In developing his theories he may also have had the help of his Portuguese father-in-law, who was another cartographer.

Like many sailors of his time, Columbus was fascinated with the problem of finding the sea route to the Indies, but at some point Columbus began to evolve his own special theory of how to get there.

A number of different things seem to have combined to help him form his theory. Columbus had visited Iceland, and there perhaps he had heard about the discoveries of the Vikings—for the people still told stories of their voyages in the Atlantic. Also, after his marriage in 1478 he lived for a time on the Portuguese island of Madeira, and he may have seen evidence there of plants and objects washed up on the beaches from the far west—even beyond the Azores.

But though people might suspect that there was land to the west, not even Columbus' famous brother Bartholomew had any positive knowledge of what, or exactly where, that land was. This was what Columbus set out to discover.

Columbus was modern enough to believe that the world was round, but he grossly underestimated its size. As a result he was convinced that the mysterious land to the far west was some part of Asia—probably Japan—and that the sea route to the fabulous Indies lay not south and east round Africa as most people supposed, but directly west across the Atlantic.

Columbus began trying to raise support to finance an expedition to prove his theory, but without success. The Portuguese, to whom he applied first, did not accept his

calculations; and the kingdom of Spain at first turned him down also, possibly because they were busy fighting a war against the Moors of Granada. Columbus persisted in his efforts, however, and at last, in 1492, was able personally to lay his plans before the king and queen.

As negotiations had been taking place for some time behind the scenes, Columbus expected the interview to be a mere formality. In fact he nearly ruined everything by his own extravagant demands for recognition and reward. He tried to insist on being made an admiral and viceroy of all the lands he discovered, besides receiving a tenth of all the profits of the voyage. However, agreement was eventually reached, and preparations could at last begin.

Then began a flurry of activity. Considering the length and danger of the voyage, preparations were carried out at lightning speed. The Spanish king provided Columbus with his flagship, the *Santa Maria*, and two thirds of the money he needed. Two more ships and the rest of the money were put up by Columbus' partner, Martin Alonso Pinzon. Pinzon came from the small town of Palos on the estuary of the river Odiel in south-western Spain, and this town also supplied the seamen for all three vessels. The idea of the voyage seems to have filled the population with dread. For though educated people were convinced that the world was round, the mass of the population were not educated and were far from convinced. To them the world was a flat plate and to sail too far westward was, they thought, to risk sailing right over the edge or at the very least into a region of total darkness beyond the setting sun.

By the late summer of 1492 the three ships destined to make the voyage were ready. By modern standards they were tiny. The royal ship, the *Santa Maria*, was about 100 feet long and a little under 100 tons. The others, the *Pinta* and the *Nina*, were trading vessels belonging to the Pinzons and were smaller with only about 50 and 40 tons displacement respectively. The whole expedition numbered little more than a hundred men, of whom at least a third were soldiers. Columbus, as admiral, sailed in the *Santa Maria*, Martin Pinzon commanded the *Pinta* and his brother Vincente the *Nina*.

On 2 August, scarcely three months after the agreement had been signed, the little flotilla set sail into the Atlantic. A week later they reached the Canary Islands, and there they were forced to remain a month while repairs were made to the *Pinta*'s steering gear. However, by early September all was ready again.

If Columbus's theory was right the Indies lay only about fifteen hundred miles west of Spain, or no more than two weeks' sailing from the Canaries.

Hopes ran high when they were eleven days out from the Canaries, for they began to find quantities of seaweed and numerous crabs floating in the water, both of which were taken as signs that land was not far away. They were wrong. In fact they had sailed into an outlying part of the Sargasso Sea, an area of calm water where masses of floating weed grows on the surface.

Another week passed, then another, and as tension began to mount among the crew there were several false alarms as over-optimistic look-outs mistook clouds on the horizon for land.

After travelling for over a month, nothing could hide the fact that wherever the Indies might be they were not where Columbus had said they were, and there were signs of mutiny. Somehow, however, Columbus managed to put new confidence into his men, and at once it was rewarded.

The very next day, 11 October 1492, they came across the first really definite signs of imminent landfall: a fresh tree-branch floating in the water, birds flying overhead, floating pieces of wood which looked as if they had been shaped and whittled by metal. That evening they made out an unmistakable coastline ahead, and dawn revealed a beautiful green island, covered in thick forests.

Columbus named the island San Salvador (it is now also known as Watlings Island). It belongs to the Bahama group of islands.

Despite the fact that nobody could be less like the fabled Mongol overlords of the East than the friendly but obviously primitive islanders, Columbus remained absolutely convinced that he had reached Asia — probably Japan. So for three months the fleet sailed back and forth searching for the Asian mainland which Columbus was sure he would eventually find. Despite his efforts, and though we usually say that Columbus discovered America, in fact he found no mainland at all — only two more beautiful islands, Cuba and Hispaniola. On Hispaniola the *Santa Maria* ran aground and had to be abandoned, but this was not such a disaster as it seemed for the sailors soon noticed that the islanders had plentiful supplies of gold, which they did not appear to value very highly.

This was obviously very promising as far as trade was concerned, for the next best thing to finding a new way to the source of the spice traffic was to find a cheap supply of gold to buy spices with in the ordinary way.

Columbus decided to build a stockade and leave a party of men behind to collect gold. He sailed for home, arriving there after a very stormy voyage, early in March 1493.

Columbus had not found the sea route to the Indies. Instead, in the space of a few months, the world the Europeans knew had become an immeasurably bigger and more exciting place. It was a discovery which would bring first enormous power and then ruin to Spain.

And of course, Columbus's mistake has left us with two lasting oddities: we still call the island chain he discovered the West Indies and the original inhabitants of the Americas "Indians".

Marco Polo goes to China

In the middle ages the world seemed both a smaller and a larger place than it is now. Smaller because so much of it remained undiscovered. Larger because travel took so long that what today is a quick journey by sea, land or air, then lasted months or years.

Very little was known in Europe about the East—Asia, India, China and beyond. These areas were unexplored, unvisited and unmapped. Strange and barbarous people were thought to live there—worshipping strange and dangerous gods. However, these areas produced the silks and spices that Europe prized so much and as a result, European rulers began to establish trading relations including protection for their merchants, while travel and trade increased. Most of the trade in these eastern goods came through Venice on the Adriatic coast and by the thirteenth century it had become a rich and powerful city.

When Marco Polo set out on the first stage of a journey in 1270, he was simply following a family tradition, even though this particular journey was to become one of the most famous and important ever made. His father Niccolo and his uncle Matteo Polo were merchants whose interests regularly took them westwards to Constantinople and the Crimea where, like many other Venetian merchants, they

specialized in the profitable trade of silks, spices and jewels.

In 1261, the two men travelled overland from the Crimea to Serai, in what we now call the southern Ukraine. This was Mongol territory, and they had only been there for a year when war broke out between the ruler of the region and one of his equally warlike Mongol neighbours. Instead of returning the way they had come, the brothers went south round the Caspian Sea to Bukhara. There they stayed for three more years, until they were contacted by envoys of the Great Khan himself—Kublai, ruler of China, who had heard of the strangers and was curious to learn more about them.

The brothers were escorted to Kublai's court: they were the very first Europeans Kublai had ever seen, and among the first ever to enter China.

Unfortunately Matteo and Nicolo kept no record of their stay at Kublai's court, but it appears that they got on well with the Khan, for they were given leave to return home on the condition that they came back as soon as possible.

It seems, also, that Kublai was impressed by their beliefs, for he gave them letters to the Pope, requesting that a hundred missionaries should be sent back with the Polos to instruct the Khan and his subjects in the principles of the Christian religion.

Two years later the Polo brothers set out once again. Surprisingly, the Pope, Gregory X, could spare only two Dominican friars for the journey. It seems that somewhere along the road their courage failed and they turned back, daunted perhaps by the many wild tales they had heard about the Mongols or the Tartars as they were called.

But the Polo brothers took with them someone destined to be far more important in history than the two wretched friars: Marco Polo, Niccolo's seventeen-year-old son.

So the Polo family continued alone—to Ayas in Syria, then overland to Hormuz on the Persian Gulf. Their plan was to take a ship from there round India, and so to China, but for some reason—perhaps they were afraid of pirates—they abandoned that plan and struck out overland.

North and east they went, through Persia, into Asia and then to the border country of modern Afghanistan.

Their way east lay across the frontier country of India. To the north lay present-day Russia, to the south the great mass of India itself. Before them lay tremendous natural hazards. First they had to climb and cross the mountain plateau of the Pamir range, which no European had ever seen before. High up in these mountains (the highest peak is over 21,000 feet) Marco noted in his diary that it was so cold that fire did not burn so brightly or give out as much heat as usual. He was right about the fire, but wrong about the cause. It was not cold, but lack of oxygen that made the flame thin and weak. Marco also recorded seeing "wild sheep of great size" in the mountains. Seven hundred years later scientists identified the *Ovis poli* species and verified his observation.

Continuing east, the party crossed the great Gobi desert. After a journey of three years they entered China, where they presented themselves to Kublai Khan at his summer palace at Shang-tu.

Truly, the Khan's palace was one of the wonders of the world. Enclosed by four miles of whitewashed stone walls about twice the height of man, it was made up of eight separate pavilions in the form of a hollow square. Each pavilion was furnished with marvels of Chinese art and craftsmanship—painted and embroidered silks, porcelain, carved lacquer, jade, rock crystal, gold.

The effect on young Marco, coming from a Europe which was still struggling to throw off the primitive styles of the Dark Ages, was almost overwhelming.

Happily, Kublai seems to have been more

than satisfied to have the Polo family back with him, and appears not to have complained at the absence of the hundred priests he had asked for. The Khan evidently found the Venetian merchants useful as diplomats. Perhaps, being totally foreign, they were more acceptable as ambassadors than Mongols, whose overlords were often fighting among themselves.

Marco made a rapid study of the Mongol language and then began his career in the Khan's service, travelling all over his vast empire. In the book he later wrote of his travels, Marco Polo makes no mention of either his father or his uncle accompanying him on any of his missions. Perhaps the senior members of the family performed independently, or perhaps they took up a semi-permanent residence at court. Sadly, they left no account of their activities. Marco, on the other hand took careful notes wherever he went: for his own and Kublai Khan's benefit.

In the course of his travels Marco saw many strange things. There was a monster for example "ten paces long and as big as a great barrel. The forelegs near the head and claws like those of a lion or hawk. The head is very big, the eyes larger than loaves. The mouth is large enough to swallow a man whole. The teeth are pointed."

Marco Polo had seen a crocodile for the first time.

Many of the things Marco saw and reported were unknown in Europe and for a long time people thought he had invented them. (When he was dying he was urged to confess all the lies he had told but retorted "I only told half of what I saw".)

In Madagascar he reported seeing giant birds "like eagles, but of the most colossal size". Generations of zoologists dismissed this as mere fantasy, but in this century remains were found in Madagascar of Marco's "elephant birds". They probably weighed about half a ton, and only became extinct in fairly recent times.

Of course, some of the wonders in Marco's book really were simple fantasies and legends that he heard on his travels—men with the heads of wolves or with heads growing from the middle of their chests were obviously not to be found even in medieval Asia. However, thirteenth-century Europeans found it just as incredible that the Chinese should use paper money (in fact they had done so for 1500 years) or burn *stones* as fuel. Coal was not used widely in Europe until the nineteenth century.

To Marco Polo the greatest wonder of all was China itself, where the arts of civilization flourished under the rule of a man whose recent ancestors had been barbaric nomad horsemen. China had a civil service, policed roads, a system of currency, cities incomparably finer than anything Europe had to show. Hangchow in eastern China had, according to Marco, three thousand public baths, twelve thousand stone bridges and hundreds of beautiful houses. At that time there may not have been as many baths, public or private, in the whole of Europe; and the streets of cities like London and Paris were undrained, their populations violent, drunken and ravaged by epidemic disease.

When Marco Polo and his companions eventually returned to Venice, in 1295, they had been away for twenty-five years. Marco Polo was now forty years old. He had travelled across Asia to Russia, China, Burma, Java, Sumatra, Ceylon, Madagascar and Persia. He was the first European to visit many of these regions and he was in many cases the last to do so for many centuries.

His account of his journeys influenced all later explorers, writers and map-makers, and his stories of the fabulous civilization of the east created a legend which fired men's imaginations and spurred them on to find a safe sea route to China so that the full wealth of the Orient could be brought to the west.

The pilgrim fathers

The Separatists lived in England, in about 1600. They were Christians who believed that religion was a matter for each person to make up his own mind about. They said that the State had no right to decide for them on matters of faith, and under the leadership of Robert Browne they began to withdraw from the Church of England. In those days this was a serious crime, and several of them were executed in 1593. In the same year an Act of Parliament was passed making it illegal to attend Separatist meetings. The penalty was banishment. Some Separatists escaped to Holland where the laws were freer, but others carried on in England as best they could.

A group of Separatists from Scrooby in Lincolnshire emigrated to Holland between 1607 and 1609. They settled in Leyden, a small town south-west of Amsterdam, where

they could live and practise their religion in relative peace. Life was hard, for they had to work as labourers. They were also worried because they were afraid a civil war about religion was coming in Holland: they would have to move again.

They decided to look for somewhere to live where they would be more peaceful. After much negotiation with a group of London merchants they managed to find money for an expedition to New England. In return they agreed to send raw materials from the new country to London, so that the merchants who gave them the money would make a profit. In addition, King James I granted them a patent to make a settlement in New England.

Seventy-four English Non-conformists from John Robinson's Church in Leyden, with twenty-eight women, left Plymouth on 23 August 1620 in the *Mayflower*, under the command of Captain Christopher Jones. The *Mayflower* was accompanied by a smaller ship, the *Speedwell*. After two days at sea the *Speedwell* developed a serious leak which forced them to put into Dartmouth for repairs. Soon afterwards they tried again, but once more the *Speedwell* proved unseaworthy. This time the "Pilgrims" as they now called themselves, were obliged to return to Plymouth to pay off the crew and transfer to the *Mayflower*. On 9 September, 102 Pilgrims left Plymouth for good.

The *Mayflower* was a three-masted, square-rigged vessel of 180 tons. She was 90 feet long, with a 64-foot-long keel. She was 26 feet across and her hold was 11 feet deep. She was armed with twelve cannon. Previously she had been used for short journeys, bringing wine to England from the Mediterranean and was rather small for long voyages. She was thought to be good enough for the North Atlantic nevertheless.

After a few days of smooth sailing the Pilgrims ran into fierce storms, during one of which the main beam amidship splintered and cracked. After much anxious discussion the Pilgrims decided to repair the beam and carry on. With the aid of a large iron screw the beam was jacked into place and secured with a post taken from the lower deck and wedged under it. There is a certain amount of mystery about why the Pilgrims were carrying such an old and heavy item as the screw. One guess is that they intended to start a printing press in New England, and this was part of the machinery.

The passengers probably slept in families, in blankets on their thin straw mattresses, on the deck or in the shallop, an open boat on deck. They ate together and what little cooking they could do was in the small brick oven on the fore-deck. After the first few days, the head winds and fierce storms that had shaken the ship caused the decks to open a little so that for the rest of the voyage their sleeping quarters were constantly wet.

One of the original men from Scrooby, William Bradford, kept a diary. In it he says that many of the Pilgrims were badly sea-sick. He also mentions a young seaman who was always swearing at them, laughing at their misery and saying that he hoped to cast half of them overboard (as corpses) before the end of the voyage. After a short time, this sailor was smitten with disease, died, and was buried at sea. Bradford writes, "Ye just hand of God on him!"

Head winds and storms continued to make rough seas and they had to continue with furled sails. During one storm John Howland was swept off the deck. He managed to grab the topsail halyards that were trailing over the side and was eventually hauled back on board. The diary relates: "Though he was something ill with it, yet he lived many years after, and became a profitable member both in church and in commonwealth (state)." One servant died and one baby boy was born, called Oceanus.

At daybreak on 9 November 1620 they sighted land "and were not a little joyful".

After some talking among themselves, the Pilgrims decided to travel south to the mouth of the Hudson river where their Patent gave them the right to settle. At midday they "fell among the dangerous shoals and roaring breakers". The ship was in trouble and the weather was turning foul. To see land after so long and then to sail away is more than most people can do. After all, for fifteen weeks they had been "lying wet in their cabbins, and most of them grew very weake and weary of the sea." They then decided to go back the way they had come along the coast. On the morning of 11 November the *Mayflower* anchored at Provincetown Harbour by Cape Cod.

Cape Cod was a cold, desolate, uninviting place and the harbour was too shallow for unloading. The *Mayflower* was anchored a mile off shore and even landing with the long boat meant wading two or three hundred yards. Sixteen men were then chosen to go ashore and scout for a suitable place to settle. They set off in full armour with their swords and muskets and were gone for three days and two nights.

In that time, they found Indians but only in the distance. They also found Indian fields and stores of corn which the Indians had buried. They also found fresh water. "We drank our first New England water with as much delight as ever we drank drink in all our lives," wrote William Bradford. On their way back one of them got his foot caught in an Indian deer trap and his friends had to release him from dangling upside down.

Some days later a second trip was arranged with thirty-four men divided between the long boat and the newly-repaired shallop. They went further south than before, past an unsuitable harbour on a freezing cold day. That harbour is still known as Cold Harbour. Later the men found a deserted Indian village and tried out some abandoned Indian canoes before they returned to the *Mayflower*.

The second mate, the only sailor who had been there before, remembered that there was a good harbour on the other headland of the bay. So, on the morning of 6 December, a third expedition set out. The going was hard and salt spray froze on their clothes "'til it was like iron". The sailors were nearly dead from cold and seasickness. Once out of the Cape, however, it got much better and they made good progress. They soon cleared Cold Harbour and landed on a beach at dusk. Here a stockade was built as a defence against wind and Indians. They all slept inside it by a big fire.

Next day most of the men travelled down the coast in the shallop while the rest formed a shore party. The only sign the shore party found was an Indian cemetery. That night they slept on the beach as before. At about midnight they were woken by terrible screams and by yelling sentries. Then a couple of musket shots went off and there was no more noise.

At five o'clock next morning, after prayers and before breakfast, the Indians attacked. First came showers of arrows and the men had to shelter behind the boat. Four of them were trapped in the stockade, two firing muskets and two loading. At last the Indians were driven off. No Pilgrim was killed. They named the place First Encounter.

By nightfall the second mate said they were very near the harbour. The sea was becoming rough and the temperature dropping again. At last they sighted the breakers that the mate said were at the harbour mouth. The boat nearly capsized on the waves before they finally landed.

When daylight came, the Pilgrims looked at the harbour and the land around it and they decided that they had found a "place they like to dwell on". For the last time they returned to the *Mayflower* and guided her to the harbour. They anchored in Plymouth harbour on 26 December 1620 and that was where the Pilgrims made their settlement.

John Gilpin

An honest draper and his wife, their wedding anniversary and a borrowed horse, these are the ingredients used by William Cowper in 1782 to make one of the most famous of all comic poems. John Gilpin's high-spirited, and tireless horse was borrowed from "his friend the Calender"—a keeper of court records. Edmonton, then in the countryside north of London, is now a suburb of the great city. The Bell Inn, alas, no longer exists.

John Gilpin was a citizen
Of credit and renown,
A train-band captain eke was he
Of famous London town.

John Gilpin's spouse said to her dear:
"Though wedded we have been
These twice ten tedious years, yet we
No holiday have seen.

Tomorrow is our wedding-day,
And we will then repair
Unto the Bell at Edmonton
All in a chaise and pair.

My sister and my sister's child,
Myself and children three,
Will fill the chaise; so you must ride
On horseback after we."

He soon replied: "I do admire
Of womankind but one,
And you are she, my dearest dear,
Therefore it shall be done.

I am a linen-draper bold
As all the world doth know
And my good friend the calender
Will lend his horse to go."

The morning came, the chaise was brought,
But yet was not allowed
To drive up to the door, lest all
Should say that she was proud.

So three doors off the chaise was stay'd
Where they did all get in;
Six precious souls, and all agog
To dash through thick and thin.

Smack went the whip, round went the
    wheels,
Were never folk so glad,
The stones did rattle underneath
As if Cheapside were mad.

John Gilpin at his horse's side
Seized fast the flowing mane,
And up he got, in haste to ride,
But soon came down again;

For saddle-tree scarce reached had he,
His journey to begin,
When, turning round his head, he saw
Three customers come in.

So down he came; for loss of time,
Although it grieved him sore,
Yet loss of pence, full well he knew,
Would trouble him much more.

Now mistress Gilpin (careful soul!)
Had two stone bottles found,
To hold the liquor that she loved,
And keep it safe and sound.

Each bottle had a curving ear,
Through which his belt he drew,
And hung a bottle on each side,
To make his balance true.

Then over all, that he might be
Equipped from top to toe,
His long red cloak, well brushed and neat,
He manfully did throw.

Now see him mounted once again
Upon his nimble steed,
Full slowly pacing o'er the stones
With caution and good heed.

But finding soon a smoother road,
Beneath his well-shod feet,
The snorting beast began to trot,
Which galled him in his seat.

So, "Fair and softly," John he cried,
But John he cried in vain;
That trot became a gallop soon,
In spite of curb and rein.

So stooping down, as needs he must
Who cannot sit upright,
He grasped the mane with both his hands
And eke with all his might.

His horse, who never in that sort
Had handled been before,
What thing upon his back had got
Did wonder more and more.

Away went Gilpin neck or nought;
Away went hat and wig;
He little dreamt when he set out
Of running such a rig.

The wind did blow, the cloak did fly,
Like streamer long and gay,
Till, loop and button failing both,
At last it flew away.

The dogs did bark, the children screamed
Up flew the windows all;
And every soul cried out; "Well done!"
As loud as he could bawl.

Away went Gilpin—who but he?
His fame soon spread around;
"He carries weight!" "he rides a race!"
"'Tis for a thousand pound!"

And still as fast as he drew near,
'Twas wonderful to view
How in a trice the turnpike-men
Their gates wide open threw.

And now as he went bowing down
His reeking head full low,
The bottles twain behind his back
Were shatter'd at a blow.

Thus all through merry Islington
These gambols he did play,
And till he came unto the Wash
Of Edmonton so gay.

At Edmonton his loving wife
From the balcony spied
Her tender husband, wondering much
To see how he did ride.

"Stop, stop, John Gilpin! Here's the house!"
They all at once did cry;
"The dinner waits and we are tired."
Said Gilpin: "So am I!"

But yet his horse was not a whit
Inclined to tarry there;
For why? His owner had a house
Full ten miles off, at Ware.

So like an arrow swift he flew,
Shot by an archer strong;
So did he fly—which brings me to
The middle of my song.

Away went Gilpin, out of breath,
And sore against his will,
Till at his friend's the Calender's
His horse at last stood still.

The Calender, amazed to see
His neighbour in such trim,
Laid down his pipe, flew to the gate,
And thus accosted him:

"What news? what news? your tidings tell,
Tell me you must and shall—
Say why bare-headed you are come,
Or why you come at all?"

"I came because your horse would come
And if I will forbode,
My hat and wig will soon be here;
They are upon the road."

So turning to his horse, he said,
"I am in haste to dine;
'Twas for your pleasure you came here,
You shall go back for mine."

Ah, luckless speech, and bottless boast!
For which he paid full dear;
For, while he spake, a braying ass
Did sing most loud and clear.

Whereat his horse did snort, as he
Had heard a lion roar,
And galloped off with all his might,
As he had done before.

Now mistress Gilpin, when she saw
Her husband posting down
Into the country far away,
She pull'd out half a crown;

And thus unto the youth she said
That drove them to the Bell,
"This shall be yours when you bring back
My husband safe and well."

The youth did ride, and soon did meet
John coming back amain,
Whom in a trice he tried to stop
By catching at his rein;

But not performing what he meant,
And gladly would have done,
The frighted steed he frighted more,
And made him faster run.

Away went Gilpin, and away
Went postboy at his heels,
The postboy's horse right glad to miss
The lumbering of the wheels.

Six gentlemen upon the road,
Thus seeing Gilpin fly,
With postboy scampering in the rear,
They rais'd the hue and cry:

"Stop thief! stop thief!—a highwayman!"
Not one of them was mute;
And all and each that pass'd that way
Did join in the pursuit.

And now the turnpike gates again
Flew open in short space;
The toll-men thinking as before
That Gilpin rode a race.

And so he did, and won it too,
For he got first to town,
Nor stopp'd till where he had got up
He did again set down.

Now let us sing: Long live the king!
And Gilpin long live he!
And when he next doth ride abroad,
May I be there to see!

The Indies at last

If you have read the story of Christopher Columbus you will already know how anxious the seamen of the fifteenth century were to discover the sea route to India—the source of the most valuable trading commodity of the age, spices. Some held that the shortest route would be found by sailing west—an error which led directly to the discovery of the Americas by Columbus. But the Indies were still the chief goal, and while Columbus sailed westward for Spain, the Portuguese continued to probe the east,

working down the coast of Africa, looking for the point where they could turn the corner towards the Indies.

That moment seemed close when, in 1487, Bartolomeu Dias rounded what *he* called the Cape of all the Storms, but which the king of Portugal insisted should be renamed the Cape of Good Hope. A mutinous crew forced Dias back almost immediately, but clearly he had pointed the way for a new voyage of discovery.

Surprisingly, it was ten years before such

an expedition was organized and equipped and when it was ready, it was led not by Dias but by a rival captain, Vasco da Gama.

No one knows very much about Vasco da Gama's early life, or what he had been doing before he was chosen to lead the new expedition. He was born about the year 1469 in the small sea port of Sines. Sines was not an important harbour like Lisbon but, small though it was, da Gama must have seen the merchant ships coming and going and perhaps he listened to the tales the sailors told of their adventures at sea. Before the voyage to the Indies, he had already pleased the King by capturing two enemy ships— and this may have been why the King now asked him to take command.

The voyage was carefully prepared. Vasco da Gama had four ships under his command, and though none of them was more than two hundred tons, the two largest—the flagship *S. Gabriel* and the *S. Rafael* had both been specially constructed under the supervision of Bartolomeu Dias. The two other vessels were the *Berrio*, and a small supply ship whose name has not survived. They were vessels of shallow draft which suited them to coastal waters and river estuaries, and they carried the same kind of guns as Portuguese warships of the time. Much of da Gama's route would lie in waters dominated by Arab seamen and merchants, who could be expected to resent the intrusion of Christian traders—not only a financial but a religious threat—into their sphere of influence.

They sailed on 8 July 1497, and by the end of the month they lay at anchor in the Portuguese Cape Verde islands, off the Guinea coast of Africa. The first leg of the journey had been completed successfully, and the small contribution of Dias was finished: for as well as supervising the special building before the expedition, he had accompanied the fleet to the islands as a kind of pilot.

The next leg of the journey was going to be more risky; it was also controversial. For unlike Dias, da Gama had no intention of creeping down the African coastline until he reached the Cape. Instead he set his course southwest in a kind of semi-circle, far out into the waters of the South Atlantic.

Perhaps he wanted to show he was a better and bolder navigator than Dias. Perhaps, as some said, he wished to avoid the currents in the Gulf of Guinea (though he did not bother to avoid them on his way home). Perhaps, for all his apparent conviction that the right route was eastwards, he wanted to make a reconaissance to the west—just in case the western theory was right after all.

Whatever da Gama's reasons, what resulted was a voyage of four thousand miles that lasted over three months. During this time the careful pre-departure preparations proved their worth: for the rations of da Gama's men consisted of generous quantities of ship's bread, salted beef and pork, oil, rice, cheese and fish; and they had a water ration of over a quart a day, with half as much again of wine. Of course, the rations lacked fresh vegetables and fruit, but the importance of these in maintaining health would not be recognized for centuries. Scurvy—a disease caused by insufficient fresh food—was at that time a frequent feature of long sea voyages.

The first landfall on the African coast was made on 7 November, at St Helens Bay; the Cape was sighted on 18 November, but, because of contrary winds, only rounded four days later.

Da Gama now changed his sailing tactics: for the time being there were to be no more daring feats of navigation, and the flotilla sailed northwards, following the coast of Africa. From this point on they were without their storeship. Her supplies having been exhausted and her job done, da Gama had ordered her to be broken up in Mossel Bay, shortly after they had rounded the Cape. So now they had to go ashore frequently to take on fresh water and gather provisions. Near Mozambique, a longer halt was made. Wooden ships sailing in warm tropical waters always picked up a heavy growth of weed and barnacles on their underwater planking, reducing their sailing speed and damaging the wood. Now da Gama ordered his ships to be beached and "careened". This involved hauling them ashore at high tide, pulling them over onto their sides, and scraping the planks clean. When one side was completed the ship had to be turned onto its other side, where the process was repeated.

The expedition finally reached Mozambique on 2 March, and was well received by the Sultan, who appointed two pilots to guide the Portuguese northwards—towards Zanzibar and Malindi. The local inhabitants seem to have thought da Gama's men were Muslims like themselves, for one of the pilots deserted the moment he discovered the truth. However, they reached Malindi safely on 14 April and the stage was now set for the final part of the journey.

At this point da Gama decided to revert to his former, bold tactics and sail directly across the Arabian Sea to India. His reasons may have been those of speed, or navigational pride—or more likely, he may have realized that the Christian Portuguese could not expect to sail free of attack through the approaches to Aden and the Red Sea.

So, at Malindi, a new pilot—a Hindu— was engaged, with the task of guiding them to Calicut, a town on the Kerala coast. At last, on 20 May 1498, da Gama finally attained his goal: Calicut was reached.

It was a momentous occasion. For hundreds of years Europeans had dreamed of finding the sea route to the Indies—to the fabulous lands and empires of the east which had remained virtually unvisited by westerners since the return of Marco Polo. Now the dream had come true.

Da Gama was well received; he was led through admiring and wondering crowds to the palace of the Zamorin (the Hindu ruler of the city) to whom he was presented. Soon after this, negotiations began for a trade agreement and, for a time everything went well.

But at this point the resident Muslim merchants, anxious to preserve their monopoly of the Indian trade, decided to take a hand. They quickly engineered such intrigues against the Portuguese that da Gama and his men were lucky to escape from Calicut with their lives.

Many of those lives were subsequently lost on a return journey which nearly became a disaster. With contrary winds the crossing of the Arabian Sea, which had taken only twenty-three days on the outward trip, now took three months, and there were many deaths from scurvy.

Indeed, so reduced were the numbers of the expedition that when it finally arrived back at Malindi the S. *Rafael* was burned on da Gama's orders.

Da Gama himself did not reach Lisbon until 9 September, though news of the expedition had been carried ahead of him by the other surviving ship, the *Berrio*. Despite the losses (which included da Gama's brother Paulo), the commander was given a hero's welcome and richly rewarded. For the Arabs and Moors had won only a temporary respite, not a victory. Two years after da Gama's departure from Calicut, the Portuguese were back, under Cabral, who established a trading settlement. And though this sortie was in turn driven off, and the traders wiped out, da Gama himself returned in 1502 with a punitive expedition which smashed the power of the Moors and forced the Zamorin into full trading relations with Portugal.

Within a few years the Indies trade was dominated by Portugal, and a whole string of Portuguese bases were strung out along the route to India—which, for better or worse, had at last been drawn into contact with Europe.

Sindbad the Sailor

The story of Sindbad the sailor comes from *The Arabian Nights*. No one knows exactly who wrote these tales, or even which country they came from, but they are certainly very old indeed. Some of the stories are about real people. Others, like Sindbad's, are strange and wonderful adventures, full of monsters, genii and magic.

Sindbad, who tells the story himself, was the son of a rich merchant. After his father died, he wasted all the money he had inherited. Then one day he decided he must change his way of life so he joined a trading ship and set off to seek his fortune. So began a series of voyages that were to take him to distant lands and into great dangers. This journey is the second of seven which made him one of the richest, and one of the wisest men in all Baghdad.

One day we landed on an island which was covered with fruit trees of all kinds. We walked in the fields and along the streams that flowed through them, but although there were lots of flowers and fruit trees, we

saw no people and no animals at all. Some of the sailors began to collect fruit and to pick flowers, but I took my food and wine and sat down in a shady spot near a stream that ran between two tall trees. I ate well and then fell fast asleep. I do not know how long I was asleep for, but when I woke up again, it was getting dusk and to my dismay I found that the ship had sailed without me.

I could not think what to do. Here I was, abandoned on the island, with very little hope of rescue. I climbed to the top of one of the trees and looked all around, hoping to see some sign of life—or at least to see the ship in the distance. There was nothing. The ship must have sailed hours before. On land, too, I could see only trees and flowers. Then I caught sight of something white in the distance. Hoping it might be a building of some kind, I decided to take a closer look.

As I approached it, I saw that it was a huge white dome, very white and smooth, with no openings or windows at all. I walked all round it (about fifty yards) and I was just about to touch it when a strange thing happened: darkness was suddenly all around me. I looked up at the sky in surprise and saw that a huge bird was flying towards me, blocking out all the light. I had never seen anything like it, but I remembered that I had often heard travellers talk about a miraculous bird called the Roc. It was supposed to be bigger than a whole flock of starlings and as strong as a hundred carriage horses. Terrified, I crouched closer to the white dome, but the bird kept coming towards me purposefully. It was not until it landed and settled itself comfortably on top of the white dome that I realized I was huddling for safety next to a giant bird's egg!

All night I stayed there, trying to keep as still as a stone, with the bird's great tree-trunk of a leg right in front of me. As it began to get light again I grew braver and I had an idea. I had to get away from the island somehow, and this seemed to be my only chance. Very carefully I unwound my turban and tied myself to the bird's leg. She did not seem to mind at all—in fact apart from ruffling her feathers a little and stirring in her sleep, I do not think that she even noticed what was going on.

As soon as it was daylight the bird stood up, flapped her wings twice and took off with a great upward jerk that made me unconscious. When I dared to open my eyes again we were flying so high that I could see nothing of the earth below but a faint blue haze. It could have been either land or sea or perhaps just the shadow of a cloud. I hastily shut my eyes and clung on more tightly than before.

After some time the Roc began to descend and once again I lost consciousness. The jolt of the landing brought me round and without pausing to look where we were, I untied the turban and rolled away on the ground. It was just as well that I did, for I had only just managed to get clear when the great bird snatched a serpent up in her bill and took off again. In no time, she was just a speck in the sky. Then she was gone.

The place where she had left me was surrounded on all sides with mountains so high that their tops were hidden in cloud, and so steep that it was obvious I would never be able to climb them. My terrifying journey seemed to have been in vain for, compared with this place, the island I had been so anxious to leave was like paradise.

For a time I just sat there and thought but soon I decided that I must at least explore and find out the worst. I stood up—still a bit shaky and surprised to be on firm ground—and set out. As I walked through the valley I saw that scattered among the boulders were hundreds of diamonds. Some of them were very large, and they flashed and sparkled in the bright sunshine. The sight of these made me feel more cheerful, but almost at once I saw something that changed my cheerfulness to terror: serpents. I had been so dazed after my flight that I had hardly noticed the one the Roc had snatched up.

but now in the distance I saw several of them writhing around among the stones. Even in the distance they looked big enough to swallow an elephant and I had no wish to get any closer to see their real size.

I spent the day walking about in the valley, resting from time to time when the sun got too hot. When night came, I found a cave to hide in. I closed the low entrance with a stone, leaving just a crack to let the light in. I ate some of the food I still had with me and then settled down to try to get some rest. For the second night running I was too frightened to sleep. During the day I had only seen a few of the serpents in the distance, but at night it seemed that there were thousands of them. I could hear them hissing and slithering over the ground, nosing at the entrance to my cave. I could imagine their fangs darting in and out and their long bodies winding around the stone that kept me secure.

When day came at last I had hardly the strength to move the boulder and to walk trembling into the sunshine. Even the sight of the diamonds glittering did not help me, and I walked on them almost without noticing them.

As soon as I had made sure that the serpents had returned to their daytime hiding places I sat down and almost immediately fell fast asleep. I cannot have been asleep for more than a few minutes, however, when a tremendous noise woke me up again. A large piece of raw meat had fallen next to me, apparently from the sky. As I looked, I saw several other pieces of meat falling. Peering up into the mountains, I could just make out tiny figures who appeared to be throwing the meat down. At first I could see no reason for this at all. Then an eagle, larger and stronger than any I had seen before, swooped down onto the piece of meat that had landed near me and, gathering it up in its talons, carried it off towards the mountain top. As it flew off I saw that several diamonds were sticking firmly to the meat,

embedded there with their sharp points. I followed the eagle's flight with my eyes. As it landed I saw a flurry of activity among the tiny people on the mountain tops. They seemed to be making their way to the eagle's nest and I quickly realized they were going to collect the diamonds the eagle had innocently brought them. All they had to do was to drive the eagle away from its nest while they picked the diamonds out of the meat.

"Perhaps once again a bird can help me to escape", I thought. So I collected some of the biggest diamonds I could see, put them in a leather bag with what was left of my food and prepared myself for another terrifying ride through the air.

I took a large piece of meat, tied it to my back with the cloth of my turban and lay face downwards on the ground to wait for an eagle to carry me off. I did not have to wait for long. Almost at once a bird swooped down on the meat and carried me up to his nest on the mountain.

The people I had seen from below immediately began to shout and wave their arms to frighten the bird away and as soon as it rose into the air again, they came over to where I was lying. At first they were very hostile, and accused me of trying to steal their diamonds but I soon convinced them that I had my own stones and was not interested in theirs. Indeed, mine were very much better, for I had chosen them carefully, while they had to take whatever happened to stick to the meat.

I offered one of my fine stones to the man who owned the nest I had landed in and he was more than satisfied with it. I found it hard to believe that I was safe at last; I thought that I must be dreaming and would soon wake up among the diamonds and serpents of the valley. But by the time I had told my story, eaten a good hot meal and had my first sleep for two days and nights, I knew that it had all really happened. The nightmare journey was over and I had made my fortune as well.

A journey to the wild west

As European settlers came to the United States in the eighteenth century they built up their new towns and started up their farms along the eastern coast. Gradually they moved further inland but at the beginning of the nineteenth century the great western region of North America was still unconquered and unexplored.

In 1803 the American government bought Louisiana from the French. The Missouri river flows through Louisiana and in 1804 the President, Thomas Jefferson, sent for Captain Meriwether Lewis and Captain William Clark to lead an expedition to follow the river to its source. With more settlers arriving all the time, the government was anxious to find new resources and new land to farm. They also wanted to find out more about the Indians who lived there and to see if it was possible to make an overland route to the west coast.

Lewis and Clark made immediate preparations and by the end of May 1804 they were ready to leave. The expedition was organized with military efficiency—and the rest of the party signed an agreement just as if they were off on military service.

For trading purposes their cargo included beads, spectacles, knives and paints carried in two canoes and a large barge-like boat 55 feet long. This was powered by twenty-two oars and, if there was a good wind, by a large sail. On the forward deck of the leading boat was a small cannon. Before departing Lewis wrote in his diary: "With this little fleet, although not quite so respectable as those of Columbus or Captain Cook, we are about to penetrate a country at least 3,000 miles in width on which the foot of civilized man has never trodden . . . and these little vessels contain every article by which we are to subsist or defend ourselves."

They did not make a good start to their journey up the river. Progress was slow through heavy currents and dangerous sandbanks. In addition there was a constant downpour of rain. They stopped from time to time and went ashore to hunt elk for food but they saw nothing of special interest. Then in July one of the party named Drewyer went ashore and discovered Indian camps with fires still smoking. He was joined by Patrick Gass and the youngest of the group, seventeen-year-old Private George Shannon. Together they went off to try to make contact with the Indians and bring them back to the boats.

While they were away Clark and Lewis organized a welcoming party with everyone dressed in full uniform. They waited for three days before the Indians appeared on horseback riding along the river bank, shouting and firing old-fashioned flint guns. Lewis ordered his men to act calmly and confidently and in order to show the Indians their armed strength he told York to fire a cannon. York aimed at a tree and struck it. This caused the Indians to retreat at once and Drewyer and Gass rode after them. The countryside was covered with grass more than six feet in height but at last contact was again made with the Indians and they were persuaded to return.

Lewis and Clark exchanged greetings with the Indian chief, and explorers and Indians sat down together to smoke pipes of peace. Long speeches of friendship were made and Lewis explained that they were all part of the family of the President of the United States. Finally presents were exchanged and the travellers went on their way.

Towards the end of October they arrived at the first really big Indian encampment that they had seen. This was the territory of the Mandans and here the explorers made their winter quarters. They made friends with the Indians and went with them to hunt buffalo, which at that time roamed the prairies in thousands. When winter came it was bitterly cold and the river was frozen so that their boats became encased with ice and they could not have left even if they had wanted to.

It was not until April in the following year that they were ready to sail on again. Within a week they had passed the highest point on the Missouri river that had ever been visited by a European. All around them they saw beautiful green countryside with many herds of antelope, deer and elk. However, their pleasure was soon spoiled by masses of mosquitoes and the dusty, dry, Dakota wind that burned the faces of the travellers and parched their throats.

One morning they had stopped by the river bank when they saw bear tracks. Drewyer, George Shannon and two others were on land and a boat had gone aground and overturned. Some of the cargo packed in boxes spilled into the water and would have been lost if it had not been for Saka, an Indian woman who was travelling with them. Although she had her papoose on her back she jumped into the water and pushed the boxes towards the bank, where they were rescued.

Suddenly Drewyer saw a bear in some bushes. He shouted a warning to Shannon and the other man. They fired at it but the bear came at them and Drewyer only managed to escape by running to the river and scrambling into a canoe. As the bear came close, Drewyer fired again and this time the animal fell dead. The overturned boat was righted and they continued their journey.

Gradually the country the great river flowed through changed and the weather became much colder. They were coming to the Montana bad-lands, a desert region of grey-green sagebrush. Though it was now May the temperature fell below freezing and their canoes were covered in ice. To add to their discomfort they kept passing through shallow rapids where they had to jump from their canoes into the freezing water. On 3 June they reached a point where the river divided into two streams and at this spot they made a camp.

Most of the party stayed in the camp to bury supplies of food and ammunition that they would be able to use on the return journey. Lewis went off with Drewyer, George Shannon, Joe Fields and Silas Goodrich to explore the surrounding countryside. They particularly wanted to find a waterfall which they had heard about from the Indians. After travelling for three days and covering more than sixty miles Lewis was going on alone while his friends were hunting. Suddenly he saw a great splash of colour in the sky. It was a rainbow such as he had never seen before. At the same time he heard a rumbling sound which grew louder and louder and as he paddled his canoe round a bend in the river he realized with delight that he was to be the first white man to see the great Falls of Montana. Crashing down more than ninety feet from the Rockies, they filled the sky with spray. The sunlight shining through the tiny drops of water had created the magnificent rainbow he had seen.

While the others made a camp and waited for William Clark to meet them with the boats bringing the main party, Lewis set off again to map the countryside. Not far from the river's edge he saw a buffalo and, going ashore, he was able to get close enough to shoot it. He did not see a large bear lurking in the bushes until it suddenly charged at him. Lewis ran for his life but the bear moved with great speed and caught up with him just as he reached the bank of the river. Lewis felt a blow in the back as he leaped into the water and as he scrambled into his canoe he realized that the bear had actually struck him. Fortunately it turned and lumbered off, leaving him in peace.

When Clark and Lewis met up again they found the waters of the river too shallow to take their boats. So a tree was cut down to make wheels for a cart on which their boats could be loaded. They could only manage about a mile and a half a day and after thirteen days they had covered only about eighteen miles. Their progress was slowed down still more by constant storms and occasional attacks by bears. When the winds were strong they put up their sails so that their boats could be blown along.

The next obstacle was a great canyon, nearly six miles long, through the Rockies. Mountains more than a thousand feet high towered up from the water's edge. Progress was slow and difficult and they often had to drag their boats through the shallow water. Occasionally they met Indians of the Shoshonee tribe. They were always friendly and rubbed cheeks and smoked the pipe of peace to show that they meant no harm.

When they could no longer travel by river they hid all their stores and set off over the mountains. At night it was bitterly cold and they had to huddle together for warmth. They managed to kill some birds and a wolf but saw little sign of wildlife and were soon short of food. At last, after three weeks Lewis and Clark saw a vast green plain below them. They reached Indian villages and were offered food—fish and roots boiled in watertight baskets.

There were more accidents with the canoes but the travellers eventually reached the Columbia River where they found the Pierced Nose Indians. The river widened into a lake and then narrowed into rapids which they had to shoot in heavy canoes. A storm forced them to seek shelter by the river bank and for a time they camped near a village of the Chinook Indians. When they were able to go on the travellers found the river was widening and the water becoming salt.

Lewis and Clark knew then that they had reached their goal: they had reached the Pacific Ocean. After travelling thousands of miles along rivers and over mountains they had crossed the American continent from east to west. They wrote a description of their journey and nailed it to a post in their last camp. It was found one week later by the captain of a ship called the *Lydia*, sailing up the west coast. But by then Lewis and Clark were on their way home. They left on 26 March 1807 and were back in St Louis by September.

More than three years had passed since they had set out into the unknown on their mission of exploration: they had discovered many things on their journey but above all they had proved that the west could be reached and could provide a new life for men and women of adventure who wished to follow.

The snow queen

This story was first told by the Danish storyteller, Hans Christian Andersen. Like many of Hans Andersen's stories, *The Snow Queen* is more than a simple fairytale about imaginary people in an imaginary world. Gerda's journey to find Kay can tell us something about our own lives too. See if you can find out what this is.

Once there was a hobgoblin who was a real mischief-maker. He loved to play tricks on people, and one of his best tricks was the creation of a huge mirror that reflected the world in a horrible way. It made all beautiful things look ugly, and all ugly things look even worse.

At first the mirror caused little suffering —only those unlucky people who were tricked by the goblin into looking at their reflections were made miserable by it. Then, one day, the mirror shattered. Splinters of glass, in their billions and trillions, flew all over the world. Some lodged instantly in people's eyes, and some in people's hearts. Many of these splinters are still flying about, and they are very dangerous. For if one lands in your eye it makes everything look sad and ugly and topsy-turvy, while a splinter in the heart soon turns to ice.

Not long after the hobgoblin's mirror had broken, two children named Kay and Gerda were playing together in a rooftop garden. They were great friends: Kay's family lived in one little attic, and Gerda's in another; and there was a space in between where their parents had placed two chairs and tubs of bright flowers and two rose trees which the children loved to sit under. In the summers they played outside, and in the winters they visited back and forth or waved to each other from their bedroom windows.

One winter night, when it was very cold, they were both indoors in Kay's home, listening to his grandmother. She told them that the snow falling thickly outside was a swarm of snow-white bees, and that the bees had a queen, who was called the Snow Queen.

"Where you see flowers of frost on the window, the Snow Queen has been and peered inside from her cold world. She longs to be closer to people."

Kay looked at the frost and thought of a glittering lady, peering at him with cold, bright eyes.

The winter passed, and the spring also. Summer came. Kay and Gerda, sitting under the rose trees, smelled sweet fresh air and laughed with pleasure at the fluffy white clouds that danced in the sky. Suddenly Kay put a hand to his eye.

"It hurts," he said. "Something hurts." It was a splinter of glass from the hobgoblin's mirror. "Oh, my chest," he said. "I have a pain." Another splinter had lodged in his heart.

Gerda looked at him, concerned. "What's

wrong?" she cried. "Let me look in your eye. Let me help you."

"Never mind," said Kay. "It doesn't matter. Nothing matters on a dull day like this." He reached up and tore a rose from the tree, pulling it to pieces while Gerda watched.

Summer vanished. Autumn came, and winter. Kay's heart grew cold and Gerda, who was often alone, cried to see the change in him. He was rude and sarcastic and he delighted in getting the better of all the other children. One very cold morning Kay took his sledge down to the market place. There the boys hitched their sledges to farmers' carts, and rode along until they were discovered and told to unhitch themselves. On this bitter morning, the place was crowded with carts. Suddenly a great white sledge appeared as if from nowhere. The driver was a lady dressed in white fur and she handled the sledge so beautifully that she moved in and out of the carts like a skater. As Kay watched, excitement grew in him; and he decided to tie his little sledge to the great one and take the fastest ride of his life. The driver stopped. Kay quickly tied his sledge behind. The driver, who did not seem to notice him at all, drove off.

Quickly they left the market place, and the town itself. They passed the last houses on the mountainside. So quickly did they travel, that the sledge seemed to fly through the snow and ice, while snowflakes as big as Kay's head were falling all around them. He was frightened, but he could not let go.

When the snow was so thick that Kay could no longer tell the earth from the sky, the driver stopped. She stepped down from the sledge, came to him and picked him up in her arms. Her robes were warm, but her touch was cold, so cold that the falling snow was warm by contrast. She kissed him, and her mouth was like ice. Kay recognized her suddenly.

"My grandmother told me about you,"

he said. "You are the Snow Queen. I saw you in my mind."

"Yes, I am the Snow Queen," she said. "And you must come and live in my palace. You have no choice."

She carried him to the driver's seat and covered him with robes. Then they drove on, while the snowflakes formed themselves into white birds that flew behind the sledge.

In the town, Gerda waited for Kay to come home, but he did not come. She waited all winter until the first rose blossomed.

"I must find Kay," she said then. "He is missing our roses." So she left the town, travelling in a little boat along the river.

She drifted downstream until she came to a garden gate near the water's edge.

"Perhaps someone here has seen Kay," she thought. So she landed her boat and went in through the gate. In the garden was a little house covered in flowering vines. It had green walls and red windows, a yellow door and a blue roof. At the door stood a a sweet, grandmotherly lady, wearing a flowered hat.

"Come in," she said. She was a witch, but Gerda did not know that; so she went in and talked to her about Kay. The witch was a kindly but lonely old soul, and as Gerda talked she cast a spell over her to make her forget everything. She made all the roses in her garden disappear, to prevent Gerda from remembering Kay, and Gerda stayed and kept her company.

The child spent her days playing in the garden, listening to the flowers talk among themselves; at night she slept peacefully in the little house. She might have stayed there forever, but that one day, as she was gazing at the familiar flowered hat, she noticed a painted rose that the witch had overlooked when she was making the roses disappear. Suddenly she remembered Kay and her journey, and without a word she left the little house and continued on her way.

It was autumn, and the weather was turning cold, when she met a friendly crow who thought that he had seen Kay. He led her to a palace where he said that Kay was living with a Princess. But it was not Kay. The Prince and Princess were very kind. They loaded Gerda with presents and gave her a golden coach. But they could not tell her where to find Kay.

Gerda continued travelling. Less than a day's journey from the palace, she was attacked by robbers and she found herself a prisoner, held by two men, a woman and a girl of about her own age. In the evening, the men went off somewhere, and the woman fell asleep. Gerda and the robber girl talked together. Gerda spoke of Kay, and the girl listened eagerly to her story. All through the quiet night they spoke, until the birds woke up to listen. Finally a sleepy wood-pigeon, who had been dozing on and off, raised her head and cooed.

"Kay," she murmured, "I remember. Kay is with the Snow Queen."

"Where?" asked Gerda. "Tell me where?"

"In the north. In her palace in the far north." The sleepy pigeon blinked. "The reindeer can take you most of the way."

"Do you mean our reindeer?" asked the robber girl.

"Yes," said the pigeon, "but you must set him free when he has done his journey."

Gerda and the robber girl went to where the reindeer was tethered. "Can you take me to the Snow Queen?" Gerda asked him.

"I can and I will, I can and I will, I can and I will if you let me," said the reindeer eagerly.

So the robber girl tied Gerda onto the reindeer's back and wished her a safe journey. The reindeer sped northwards, to Lapland and Finland, plunging up hillsides and down. Gerda had no idea where they were or what direction they were travelling in; she could see only the swirling whiteness around them. Her cheeks smarted and her lips were blue with cold, but she thought of Kay and her heart never failed her.

At last they came to the Snow Queen's garden, and there the reindeer said that he must stop.

"You must go alone to the palace," he said. "If I went further I should be the Snow Queen's prisoner. I'll wait here for you."

Gerda ran forward as fast as she could. Her hair flew out behind her and froze in mid-air. Her hands and her feet became numb. She saw before her a palace of ice, a harsh, inhuman place of unexpected caves and splintered towers. But she was unafraid.

She ran inside, into a great hall. There, in the centre was Kay. He was pushing and pulling at large cakes of ice. The Snow Queen, who had gone away to Denmark to arrange a violent snowstorm, had left instructions that he must arrange these pieces so that they spelled the word "Love".

"If you can do that, you will be free of me," she had told him.

When Gerda entered, Kay looked up from his task. His heart had grown so cold that he did not recognize her, but she ran to him and threw her arms around him, crying, "Kay. Poor Kay." Her warm tears fell on him and at once the splinter melted in his heart. He hugged her close and cried, and the splinter in his eye was washed away.

All at once the cakes of ice that had been obstinately lying still, resisting all Kay's efforts, moved gracefully around each other and arranged themselves into the word "Love". Kay smiled happily at Gerda, and hand in hand they left the Snow Queen's Palace. They passed through the garden, and found the reindeer waiting. Kay lifted Gerda onto the reindeer's back, and climbed up behind her. In one blink of the Northern lights, they were home again. It was summer, and the rose trees were flourishing. Gerda turned to thank the reindeer, but he, knowing he was free, had already gone.

After they had admired every rose on the trees, Kay and Gerda went inside to visit Kay's grandmother. As they stood before her, they realized suddenly that they had grown up; and they were happy at last.

The last flight of the Italia

Humberto Nobile's first airship journey across the Arctic had been a resounding success. In 1926 together with Roald Amundsen, the great Norwegian explorer, he had flown a comparatively small airship of his own design (renamed the *Norge* for the occasion) from Italy to Norway, and then across the Arctic and over the North Pole.

The first success encouraged Nobile into a much more ambitious plan; not only would he fly across the Pole, he would also explore the virtually unknown Nicholas II Land. He wanted to chart the extreme northern Canadian coastline and a large, unexplored region of Greenland. To achieve this he decided to design a new airship.

The first successful airship had been built in 1884 in France. Later, Count Ferdinand von Zeppelin designed much larger ones, with immense metal skeletons, which were used in the First World War. There were two types of airships, dirigibles (really elongated balloons with engines) and rigid airships. Nobile's airship was a rigid one. It had a hollow, cigar-shaped frame filled with bags inflated with hydrogen gas to keep it in the air. The small cabin was attached underneath.

Airships had many problems. Their engines were unreliable and the hydrogen gas caught fire easily. One of their biggest problems was staying at the right height. The hydrogen gas expanded when it was heated and contracted when it was cooled.

When it expanded it made the airship fly higher and when it contracted the ship came down again. The higher the airship rose, the less the air pressure outside became and this made the gas expand even more, taking the airship even higher. In order to prevent the airship from bursting, there had to be some way of releasing the gas. The trouble was that once the gas had gone, it could not be replaced. The airship came down but could not go up again, and this caused many disasters.

The year after his first flight, backed by the Italian Government and a public subscription, Nobile began work on a new and improved airship, to be named the *Italia*. By March 1928, the *Italia* was completed and the long preliminary journey north began.

Despite hazardous weather conditions, Nobile's expedition moored safely at King's Bay in early May. Final preparations were begun immediately. Everyone was optimistic. Surely the Arctic wastes could not provide worse weather conditions than those they had endured so far?

Nevertheless their first start on 11 May was attended by dreadful weather and ominously the *Italia* was forced back to the safety of her moorings.

They struck out once more for Nicholas II Land on 15 May. The *Italia* was carrying sixteen men including two scientists and a newspaper reporter, Nobile's dog, a wealth of scientific equipment and enough fuel for over 4,000 miles. The weather was fine and in less than three days they were back, triumphantly bringing with them a detailed survey of 1500 square miles of previously uncharted land.

Now Nobile pressed ahead with his plans to reach the Pole. He intended to land at the Pole, not simply fly over it; and the *Italia* had been specially prepared to withstand a descent onto the ice floes.

On 23 May just before 4.30 a.m., the airship left her moorings and just twenty hours later, shortly after midnight, she was over the Pole. Flags and a cross were dropped; observations were taken; radio messages were transmitted. No landing on the Pole was achieved since worsening weather once more upset Nobile's plans and after hovering expectantly for two hours, Nobile set course for King's Bay. As they laboured on southwards the weather continued to deteriorate. There was heavy freezing fog and gale-force head winds. In such conditions accurate navigation was impossible so that thirty hours later Nobile was lost. A brief radio contact with their base was made— but it only served to prove to them that they were nowhere near King's Bay. They had no clue at all as to their real position.

Ice began steadily building up on the ship's exterior surface, and nothing could be done about it. Then, at 9.25 a.m. on 25 May the elevators jammed and in order to repair them the engines had to be stopped.

At this point, Nobile made a fatal mistake. The *Italia*, with engines off, was floating like a free balloon; it was so light after burning such a weight of fuel that in the absence of controlled power, it rose. Nobile allowed it to. It rose above the fog; above the clouds to 3000 feet into brilliant sunshine, and thinner air. It was a relief to leave the fog behind but they had to be able to see the ground in order to navigate. So when the engines could be started again, Nobile dived the *Italia* through the fog once more; and in doing so he doomed her.

The ship had lost a lot of hydrogen as it rose higher and higher. Some had been released automatically as the atmospheric pressure outside had decreased. Some, warmed by the sunshine, had expanded and escaped through the valves. As the ship sank downwards again into the cooler, denser air below, the hydrogen inside contracted until there was no longer enough left to carry the weight of the ship.

Desperate efforts were made to lighten the ship; all ballast (and just about everything else within reach) was thrown overboard. It was too little and too late. The *Italia* kept sinking helplessly until it crunched sickeningly into the ice, like a huge frail toy. The impact burst open the control car. Nobile, his dog, eight of his colleagues and a quantity of equipment came tumbling out. At last the *Italia* was sufficiently lightened. She rose again at once with six crewmen still on board and disappeared from view forever: neither airship nor men were ever seen again.

The survivors started to gather their scattered provisions and equipment from the ice. Nobile was in great pain from a broken leg and arm. The others were less seriously injured but they were suffering from shock. They all realized they were completely lost.

There was a moment of hope when a radio set was found intact and Guiseppi Biagi, the operator, sent out a distress signal. But there was no reply. They had a single four-man tent in which they all huddled. Death seemed inevitable for them all. The s.o.s. had been received however, at least partially, at King's Bay, and since absolutely nothing had been heard from the airship, the s.o.s. and the fate of the *Italia* were linked. Unfortunately not enough of the message had been picked up to fix the survivors' whereabouts.

Within a day, a massive search operation started, hampered by the fact that the searchers had no idea of where the airship could be.

No further messages from Nobile's crew were received, although in fact messages were being sent continuously by Biagi. Indeed the *Italia*'s radio was working perfectly, and though Biagi's transmissions didn't get through, he could clearly hear the rescue teams talking to each other.

The days crawled by; the meagre rations stretched more thinly as the ice drifted steadily south-east, taking Nobile's men further and further away from the area the searchers were likely to cover. At this point they decided to try a last desperate iniative. Three of them left the group and struck out across the ice towards the point where they believed the nearest land to be. The others waited with increasing despair. Biagi kept transmitting invariably without being answered. Their radio on the other hand was still receiving more and more gloomy bulletins, describing the search for themselves.

Then, when there was no hope left on either side, on 9 June (the sixteenth day adrift), King's Bay at last picked up a faint message from Biagi. This time they got his position, too.

The lost expedition went wild with relief, as the evening broadcast told them that help was on the way. But the continual drift of the ice was difficult to measure accurately, and for two weeks ten aircraft criss-crossed back and forth over the new search area. When at last they were spotted, it was 13 June. The following day Nobile was evacuated.

Fate nonetheless still had some tricks to play on them. When the Swedish rescue pilot returned for the next load he was grounded by engine trouble and he too became imprisoned with the others. It was not until 12 July that the last man was taken off the ice.

The same day, a Russian ice-breaker accidentally stumbled across two of the men who had set out for help. Their companion, the Swedish scientist Malingren, had died weeks before: the seventh casualty of Nobile's disastrous adventure, but not the last. There was one last piece of tragedy left. The Arctic is a dangerous place both for rescuers and for those needing rescue and the aircraft of the period were risky in themselves. One rescue aircraft vanished without trace on its way to King's Bay to join the hunt. The six men on board included the man who, with Nobile, had achieved the first flight over the North Pole: the great Roald Amundsen.

Mungo Park and the Niger

Everybody knew there was a river called the Niger which flowed through the centre of Africa. People had always known that; the ancient Greeks had known it, and so had the Romans. The trouble was, very few people had actually seen it, and even those who said they had seemed unable to agree about it. Some said it flowed east and others that it flowed west, some insisted it was a branch of the Nile, others that it was a branch of the Congo. One expert was certain that it ran into the Atlantic Ocean, a second that it disappeared into the Sahara Desert, a third that it ended—or perhaps began—in a great lake. Even the people who lived on its banks, and sometimes made journeys to the coast where they met Europeans, could say little about it. It was *N'ger-n-gereo*, the Great River, the River of Rivers, and as far as they were concerned, once it had passed the town or village where they lived, it probably flowed on for ever.

Fever-ridden swamps, ferocious animals, bandits who robbed and sometimes killed strangers had all prevented Europeans from travelling very far inland. The few who had tried had either died or been forced back. In 1795, Mungo Park, the son of a poor Scottish farmer, was sent out to succeed where others had failed. He was twenty-three years old, tall, with flaming red hair. He had already sailed to Sumatra as a ship's doctor. Now, for fourteen shillings (70p) a day and £200 for his expenses, he had been set down alone on the western edge of Africa. His task was to find out once and for all where the River Niger was, and whether it flowed east or west.

In June, he reached Pisania, on the Gambia River, the last outpost of the Africa Company. Before the end of the month he had caught his first fever, but on 2 December, when the rainy season was over, he set out. He had with him a servant, an interpreter and a boy named Bemba, a horse and two donkeys, beads and tobacco with which to buy supplies, a few spare clothes, a compass and one or two other instruments, two muskets and two pistols, and a large umbrella. Four traders from the interior joined him and stayed with him for a time.

As he and his companions travelled deeper into this malaria-ridden country, its low hills and thick forests seemed to become more and more oppressive. By day it became so hot that rocks would burn uncovered skin. By night it was often too cold for sleep. Sometimes there were furious downpours of rain. In addition, they might be attacked at any time by raiding, slave-gathering parties of Moors from the north.

Slowly, Mungo Park travelled eastward, moving from village to village. The villages were clusters of mud-walled huts, and each one was guarded by the masks and gaudy costumes of witch-doctors and priests. He would stand and wait beside these until someone offered him food and shelter. As time went by, he became dirtier and more ragged, his red hair and beard grew wild about his face, and he received fewer and fewer of these invitations. Instead, people either ignored him or insulted him.

On Christmas Day he met his first bandits. They pretended to come from the king whose country he was crossing and told him that as a stranger he had to pay a toll. They went through his luggage and made off with half of everything he owned. From now on, the same thing happened to him in almost every town or village that he came to, for he had reached lands where the Moors of the north were strong. But everywhere the Africans, who were sometimes ruled by the Moors and always afraid of them, helped him and gave him food.

One night, as he was sleeping on the floor of a hut in a town he calls Funingkedy, he heard shouts and screams, the sharp crack of musket-fire, and in the distance the terrified lowing of cattle. He scrambled up on the thatched roof and saw, through the moonlight, a herd of bullocks thundering towards the town. Behind them five Moors on horseback raced to and fro, shooting as they came, their white robes fluttering. The townsfolk, meanwhile, ran to and fro or gathered by their walls, too frightened or surprised to fight. Just outside the town the Moors stopped the herd, took from it sixteen of the best cattle and drove them off at a gallop, their dismayed owners watching silently.

Mungo Park pushed on. He visited Tarra, where Major Houghton, the one man who had preceded him, had either been murdered or had died of starvation. At the town of Deena he was robbed again, this time by the four merchants who had been his companions since the beginning of the journey! His servants now wanted to turn back, but, he tells us, "I resolved to proceed alone".

In the moonlight, more danger threatened. He speaks of "the roaring of wild beasts". It was man, however, who proved more dangerous than any animal. Mungo Park next fell into the hands of a cruel ruler named

Ali, who took everything he had, stripped him of most of his clothes and kept him a prisoner, forcing him to drink from the same trough as his cattle.

After a month, Ali released him, but kept his boy, Demba, to be his slave. Not surprisingly, Mungo Park's interpreter refused to go any further. He was now completely alone as he made his way deeper into unknown territory. He was very thin by this time, a gaunt man, six feet tall, with tangled hair and a huge red beard, travelling on and on under the sun and heavy skies of Africa. All he had left were two pairs of trousers, two shirts, two waistcoats, two handkerchiefs and a pair of boots. Almost the whole time he was shivering from fever. He had no food and no drink. Once, only rain saved him from dying of thirst; once he was kept from starvation by a motherly African woman who gave him a dish of *couscous*. Yet still he had no thought of giving up.

In the end, this courage was rewarded. He joined a small caravan and soon found himself travelling through cultivated land. Then, in the distance, he saw the smoke of cooking fires, the deep brown of mud walls. It was the town of Segu, capital of a small state called Bambara. One of his companions suddenly pointed and called out:

"See the water!"

There before them, dividing the town, was a river. He saw it, he says "with infinite pleasure", for it was indeed "the long sought for majestic Niger, glittering in the morning sun, as broad as the Thames at Westminster, and flowing slowly *to the eastward*". It was 20 July 1796. He had solved part of the puzzle.

He journeyed on, following the river's course. His horse at last collapsed and he threw away its collar and let it go. A week later, describing himself as "worn down by sickness, exhausted with hunger and fatigue, half naked, and without any article of value by which I might procure provisions, clothes or lodging", he at last decided

he could go no further; he must return to the coast.

Now he was completely at the mercy of the villagers he met. Some spat at him, some threw stones, some laughed and jeered. Others, however, proved kinder, giving him food and shelter. One day, he heard the neighing of a horse—and there was his old companion, trotting towards him! He was not entirely friendless, therefore, when he limped on. But he was still attacked by the shivering fits of fever.

On he went, clambering up the steep and rocky hills, pushing his way through thickets in which lions and other savage beasts often lurked, swimming the swift, narrow rivers which crossed his path, terrified every day of the possibility of being robbed and murdered.

Bandits in fact took from him almost everything he had left. They even threatened him with a sharp knife—then cut the buttons off his waistcoat and stole them. They left him a shirt and a pair of trousers—and just before riding off, threw him back his hat. Had they but known it, this was now the most valuable object he owned, for it was inside its crown that he kept all his notes.

Soon afterwards, he met a small caravan leading a party of wretched slaves for sale to the coast. The slave-trader, however cruel to the men he had chained up, proved friendly to this stranger and helped him on his way. Two months later, on 11 June 1797, Mungo Park walked once more into the village of Pisania, where his journey had begun almost exactly two years before.

If you look at a map of Africa, you will discover just why people were for so long confused about the great river Niger. Rising in the marshes of eastern Mali, it flows east for several hundreds of miles before looping round to flow south to the coast. Though Mungo Park's journey into the interior solved some of the problems, it was many years before all the secrets of the Niger were finally revealed.

Darwin and the Beagle

Ever since his boyhood in Shrewsbury, Charles Darwin, the son of a doctor, had loved wildlife of all kinds. While he was at Cambridge university (from 1828 to 1831) his greatest pleasure had been collecting insects.

One day after he had left the university he returned home to find a letter waiting for him from Professor Henslow, his lecturer in botany at Cambridge. The letter mentioned that Captain Robert Fitzroy, commander of the *Beagle*, was going on a voyage of scientific discovery round the world and needed a naturalist to add to his team of scientists.

At first Dr Darwin would not agree but he told his son, "If you can find any man of common sense who advises you to go I will give my consent." Fortunately for Charles Darwin his uncle, Josiah Wedgewood, visited Shrewsbury at that time and stated his belief that it would be wise to accept the chance to go on the *Beagle*. So the next day Darwin set off for London to be interviewed by Captain Fitzroy. To his delight Darwin was accepted and given the duties of studying geology and collecting animals of all kinds, including sea ones.

On 24 October 1831 at the age of twenty-two, Charles Darwin arrived at Plymouth ready for his great adventure. The *Beagle* made two attempts to sail but was driven back by gales and storms in the English Channel. At last on 27 December the ship left Plymouth with a commission to make a general scientific survey of coasts and harbours all over the world.

By January they were approaching the Canary Islands and on 6 January they reached Teneriffe. There was a cholera epidemic in the town, however, and so they could not go ashore. Ten days later they anchored at Porto Praya in St Jago, the

chief island of the Cape Verde Group. Darwin rode about the island on horseback and noticed that the commonest bird he saw was the kingfisher. When he had the chance he observed sea creatures, including the sea slug which he watched staining the water with a purple fluid. He was interested too in the way the octopus could change its colour like a chameleon and could also stain the water with a dark brown fluid.

By 16 February they were anchored near the island of St Paul and once again Darwin was able to go ashore to explore and make notes on the wildlife. He found only two kinds of birds: the booby and the noddy. Both birds were very tame and seemed completely unaware of possible danger. Darwin was able to walk so close to them that he could easily have either caught or killed them. He was amused to see how a crab was able to steal a fish from the nest of one of these birds.

Then came the voyage across the Atlantic to Brazil, which they reached on 29 February. Darwin was excited to get his first sight of the tropical South American forest and delighted to see the beauty of the plants, flowers and trees. The noise from the millions of insects in the forest was so loud that Darwin claimed to be able to hear it when he was on the *Beagle* several hundred yards from the shore.

When he went ashore, however, he was soon to discover the savagery of the tropical climate. He had been wandering about enjoying the exciting sights of the jungle and looking out for unusual insects and plants. He decided it was time to return to the ship and was making his way back to the landing stage when it started to rain. Darwin ran to shelter under a tree but the rain was so strong that it forced its way through the branches and ran down the trunk like a river. By the time he reached the *Beagle* Darwin was soaked to the skin.

Everything he saw in the forest was strange and wonderful. The birds were more

brilliantly-coloured than any European bird and giant-sized butterflies flitted among the tropical blooms. There were stones turned shiny black by metal oxides in the rivers and a fish called the Diodon that could blow itself up like a balloon. From the heights of Punta Alta Darwin was able to enjoy a view of the whole harbour of Bahia Blanca, and while on an expedition to look for fossils of extinct animals he saw the tracks of a puma or mountain lion. This big cat liked trees and high places and Darwin kept on the alert in case of danger, but although he saw some skunks there was no sign of mountain lions.

They arrived at Bahia Blanca on 2 August and Darwin found the town in a state of constant excitement because of an expected invasion by enemy tribes. Captain Fitzroy agreed that Darwin should go ashore and make his way overland to Buenos Aires, a distance of about four hundred miles.

The *Beagle* sailed a week later and Darwin was left to explore the coast and prepare for his long journey. Amongst the clay and rock Darwin searched for fossils and one day he made a find. Close together on the beach he was excited to see the bones of nine giant creatures of a prehistoric age. One collection of bones that especially interested him were those of an extinct type of horse. They proved that there had once been horses in South America although none was left when the first European explorers came in the sixteenth century.

With a gaucho guide Darwin set off for Buenos Aires and eventually reached the Sierra de la Ventana, a mountain where, as far as Darwin knew, no European had ever been before. Like the forests, the mountain climate was new and strange. By day it was hot but the nights were so cold that when he woke in the morning Darwin found that the dew on the saddle cloths under which he slept was frozen.

They crossed a dry, grassy plain seeing few signs of life. Then one day they saw a cloud of dust in the distance and realized that Indian horsemen were approaching. Fortunately they were friendly and were going to fetch salt for their people. (In his notebook Darwin wrote that the Indians were very fond of salt, their children sucking it like sugar.) Continuing his journey, Darwin reached a small settlement where a troop of soldiers joined him. They reached Buenos Aires on 20 September and Darwin stayed there for a week before setting out once more. This time he was bound for Santa Fé, three hundred miles away.

For this stage of the journey, Darwin travelled in a bullock waggon along roads so ruined by downpours of rain that they could only move along at about one mile an hour. He rested at Bajada for five days and used the time to explore the surrounding countryside. At the bottom of some cliffs he was delighted to find an assortment of fossils, including the shells of sea creatures and sharks' teeth. Yet the nearest ocean was more than a hundred miles away. Again he heard rumours of dangerous animals (this time jaguars) but although he saw deep scratch marks in the barks of trees where they had sharpened their claws, he did not see the animals themselves.

The journey overland had made Darwin unwell and on 12 October he decided to return to Buenos Aires by river in a one-masted boat called a *balandra*. It was a voyage full of interest for the young naturalist. On the river bank he might glimpse a capybara (a large rodent, rather like a guinea-pig) and, skimming the water, strange birds such as the scissor-beak with its long, pointed wings and a beak that Darwin described as being "flat and elastic as an ivory paper cutter".

By December Darwin had joined the *Beagle* again and was sailing to Port Desire on the coast of Patagonia. There was always a great deal to observe but one evening he saw one of the strangest sights of the voyage: a great mass of butterflies, so great

that it darkened the sky, flew over the boat. It seemed to be raining butterflies. Darwin thought they had probably been blown out to sea by the wind.

It was an exciting experience to sail through the Strait of Magellan at the very southernmost tip of South America, and then north along the coasts of Chile and Peru. After stopping at Valparaiso and getting a glimpse of the Andes mountains in the distance, Darwin's next opportunity to go ashore and explore was when they reached the Galapagos Islands, on the Equator. On one island he saw two tortoises eating a piece of cactus. As he approached one gave a loud hiss before pulling its head into its shell while the other glared and then lumbered off. Apart from the tortoises he saw turtles and black lizards more than four feet long. He was amazed at the birds, which were so tame that he could have caught one by dropping his hat on it. On one occasion Darwin was resting and holding a pitcher of water when a thrush perched on it and began to drink.

The *Beagle* went on to Tahiti and then to Australia and New Zealand. By 19 July they were at the Ascension Islands and Darwin received a letter from his sisters telling him that Professor Henslow had received his collection of fossils and that these were causing great interest in England. He was so pleased that he wrote, "After reading this letter I clambered over the mountains of Ascension with a bounding step and made the volcanic rocks resound under my geological hammer."

The *Beagle* crossed the Atlantic to stop briefly in South America again before completing the voyage round the world via the Azores. On 2 October 1836 Darwin went ashore at Falmouth after a voyage that had lasted nearly five years. This great journey of discovery gave Charles Darwin a unique knowledge of the wildlife of the world and prepared him for his great work, the writing of his famous book *The Origin of Species*.

The great trek

White people first settled in Southern Africa around the town of Cape Town four hundred years ago. Most of them came from Holland and worked for the Dutch East India Company. Cape Town became an important city on the shipping route to India.

As time went on, the people called themselves *Afrikaaners* (Dutch for Africans) or *Boers* (the name which distinguished them from English settlers). They had strong views about how they should live and how they should treat the native Africans. For the Boers, the great difference was that they were Christians chosen by God, but the Africans were pagans, and only to be looked down on. They were so convinced of this that when missionaries and other Europeans preached that Africans could be Christians and all people are equal in the sight of God, they were prepared to go away from the Cape into unknown and dangerous country in order to find lands where they could settle and live according to their beliefs.

Both the Boers and the native Africans

counted their riches by the numbers of sheep and cattle which they owned. When it came to fighting, the Boers had guns and ammunition. The African armies were far larger but were only armed with spears. They were also in some cases very well trained, having learned from the Portuguese in the north.

The first man to lead a small group of Boers out of the Cape Colony was Louis Tregardt.

The method of travel worked out by Tregardt's people was followed by all the Boers who made the Trek. They travelled in families. Each one owned a large wagon like a very old-fashioned caravan. Inside the wagons were the beds on which the women and children slept with all the storage space they had underneath the beds. They also had to take farming implements, seeds and so on, in case they found a suitable place to settle, besides guns and ammunition. Each wagon was drawn by sixteen oxen, led by an African servant and urged on by a man with a very long whip.

What held the families together both on this first expedition and later, was the belief that God watched over them. Especially at the start, the people were trekking into completely unknown, unexplored country, not as explorers but as families. The men had to be constantly on the look-out for lions, crocodiles and other wild beasts who would eat the livestock. They had to find food as they went along and very often they had to spend days looking for a suitable ford across rivers.

Following Louis Tregardt, came the main body of the Boers led by two men, first Andries Potgieter, and later another group with Piet Retief.

The first group, under Potgieter, made for the Waal, one of the rivers to the north of the colony. As they reached the river they were faced by a strong and powerful African tribe called the Matabele. The King of this tribe ruled over 30,000 square miles of country. He was friendly with missionaries but had no wish to see his land taken over by white people.

An army of Africans was sent out with instructions to kill all the white males and bring back their women and girls. After a fierce battle, fifty-three white men, women and children were killed, while five wagons, seventy-four head of cattle and twenty-three horses were carried off.

Potgieter, as leader, realized that they would have to defeat the Matabele if their lands were ever to be secure. He decided to stand and fight the Matabele forces.

To protect themselves, the Boers lashed their wagons together in what they called a *laager*. They formed a strongly protected square. The Boers fired their guns from behind it but the African spears could not penetrate. Although this sounds very strong, Potgieter had only thirty-three men and seven boys to meet the enormous African army. When the Matabele came within sight there were over five thousand of them.

The African army charged the *laager*, hoping to storm it. They were beaten back three times, however, by the murderous fire of the Boers' guns. After the third charge had failed, the Matabele left, taking all the Boers' cattle with them but leaving behind five hundred dead.

Only two of the Boers were killed and only fourteen were wounded. They were obliged to move, however, and wait for assistance. This came from more and more people trekking north from the Cape colony. Among them was a man called Gert Maritz.

The majority of Boers, who by 1837 numbered up to one thousand families, each with a wagon and livestock, wanted to go northeast. This meant crossing a fierce looking range of mountains called *The Dragon*. Small expeditions had already found passes that would take ox-wagons. More important, they had heard that on the other side was a very rich land with a port as well. This group of Boers found their leader in Piet Retief.

The first thing Retief did to make the trek less dangerous was to make treaties with neighbouring African chiefs. Among those he tried to make a peaceful settlement with was the King of Zululand, Dingaan. This King ruled most of the land beyond what would be the northern border of the new Boer settlement. At first Dingaan told Retief that this land would be available.

Retief was amazed at what he saw of the Zulu capital. There was a large area, two miles in circumference, enclosed by a very high wooden fence. Inside were nearly two thousand wooden huts, six rows deep and each capable of holding twenty warriors. In the centre was a large empty space where military exercises and ritual dances took place. The King's palace was a spherical shape supported by twenty-two pillars entirely covered with beads. The floor was perfectly smooth and shone like a mirror.

Dingaan was extremely suspicious of the approaching white men. Someone wrote at the time that Dingaan said, "I see that every white man is an enemy of the black, and every black man an enemy of the white; they do not love each other and never will." He was determined to defeat the Boers by lying to them and then wiping them out in one massacre. To begin with he asked Retief to go on a raid against a neighbouring tribe, as a token of friendship, and take back some royal cattle which had been stolen. After that, he said, he would give them the land.

When he returned successfully to the King, Retief had no idea of his real intentions. He chose sixty-seven men and rode cheerfully into the King's enclosure. Negotiations went on for a few days and Retief's men were well entertained. Then on the last day, 6 February 1838, as Retief and his men were ready to go, they received a message from the King asking them to assemble on the parade ground so that he could say good-bye. They left their horses at the town gate and were asked to give up their arms before approaching the King.

They sat around the King watching a fine display of native dancing. What they did not realize was that the large circle of dancers was gradually closing in on them. Suddenly, the King leaped up shouting: *Bulalani anatagati!* ("Kill the wizards!") The Boers tried to defend themselves with their hunting knives but the situation was hopeless. They were overpowered, bound with raw-hide thongs and dragged to the hill of execution.

Dingaan now sent his army to massacre the rest of the Boers. Though the Zulu army was eventually beaten off; five hundred members of the Great Trek were killed during the night of 16–17 February 1838.

The double massacre left the Trekkers leaderless, miserable, with desperately wounded men to care for and innumerable women and orphans to look after. They were still in great danger from the Zulus, who realized now that they must completely destroy the Boers or be driven out of their own land. It was at this point that the Trekkers were most united and most needed their religious belief that God would protect them.

Maritz became their leader for a time and Potgieter crossed the mountains to provide help. Their greatest good fortune however was to find another leader in Andries Pretorius. He brought with him more people from the south who wished to settle near the port of Durban. He worked very hard and was a particularly good military leader. It was he who commanded the last battle against the Zulus, when the massacre of Retief and his men was avenged by the deaths of over three thousand Zulus. When the Boers eventually reached Dingaan's capital they found that the town was burning and Dingaan had fled.

In spite of these victories, the Boer Trek to find new lands did not end until 1852, when the British finally acknowledged the Boer's right to govern themselves in the lands they were occupying.

Flight across the Atlantic

In the 1920s aviation was in its "heroic age". People still talked about the "conquest of the air". It was taken for granted that such a conquest involved an element of fatal risk and personal heroism. Gradually, as the conquest was achieved its progress was outlined by brilliant landmarks. One of the most famous was the first non-stop flight between New York and Paris.

This particular flight was the idea of a Frenchman named Raymond Orteig, a hotel manager in New York. In 1920 he promised a prize of $25,000 "to the first aviator who crosses the Atlantic in a land or water aircraft (heavier than air), from Paris or the shores of France to New York, or from New York to Paris or the shores of France without stopping." The distance was about 3,600 miles.

The first attempt was made on 21 September 1926 by Captain René Fonck, a French flying ace from the First World War. His aircraft was a large silver bi-plane especially designed by the famous aeronautic engineer Sikorsky. It was luxuriously equipped and furnished and had a crew of four. It was so overweight however that it failed to reach take-off speed, crashed and exploded. Fonck and his navigator escaped unharmed, but the two other members of the crew were burned to death.

Fonck's disaster did not deter several other fliers, American and European, from making preparations. Fonck himself also announced that he would try again. Nearly all these fliers were famous men with virtually unlimited financial backing.

But an unknown young man committed himself to the race, too. He was Charles Lindbergh, twenty-five years old, an ex-

71

flying cadet who was then an airmail pilot.

Sometimes when Lindbergh was flying over well-known country with no navigation problems, "nothing to match oneself against", as he wrote later, he "used to dream about being really able to stay up in the air and keep on flying. . . . I would think of myself like a man on a magic carpet who could fly anywhere in the world." With enough fuel, he thought, maybe he could even fly non-stop from New York to Paris!

Gradually Lindbergh's dream became more real. Enough fuel, he decided, was the first priority. The plane should be stripped of every ounce of unnecessary weight to allow a maximum load of fuel and the minimum overall weight. For this reason Lindbergh was convinced that a single-engined plane might be the safest. For a two or three engined aircraft with a full load of fuel would not have enough power to continue if one of its engines failed. Naturally the plane should be stripped of unnecessary comforts like upholstery in the cabin. The instruments for navigating would have to be reduced to the bare essentials; only emergency rations would be carried. The crew must be reduced to one—himself. It would mean staying awake for almost two days and two nights but he believed he could do it. Lindbergh needed financial support for such a major flying project and it took him a long time to persuade his first supporters that a single-engined, single-man flight offered the best chance of success.

Then there was the problem of getting the plane he wanted. Several major air companies simply refused to deal with him on what they considered a mad adventure. Only the small company Ryan Airlines agreed to build him a plane to his specifications and at a fraction of the price any one else would have charged. It seemed almost *too* good, but eventually it all proved to be true. The aircraft would be the Ryan model M-2 re-designed to give a range of 4,000 miles, with a Wright engine.

Once he had the plane, Lindbergh had to make agonizing decisions concerning the equipment he would carry. He had to sacrifice his comfort and even his safety to the need to carry more fuel. So, no radio or sextant; he decided to navigate by observation only. The plane was designed to weigh 5,180 pounds fully loaded, including the 170 pounds assigned to Lindbergh's body. In fact the plane would exceed that weight by 135 pounds since the fuel tanks had come out oversize. The aircraft was all metal and painted in black letters on its side was the name *Spirit of St Louis*. Lindbergh was a pilot on the St Louis to Chicago route and the money he needed to finance his flight had all come from people living in that city.

When Lindbergh began to test his plane with increasing loads he found its performance nearly perfect. Nevertheless his chances of being the first to get away for Paris were very small. Other fliers were preparing for the flight too, apparently at a faster rate than he. They were, Commander Noel Davis, Commander R. E. Byrd and from Paris, Captain Nungesser. But then, a series of unlikely accidents prevented them all from leaving.

Although Lindbergh was ready by 16 May, bad weather caused a delay and it was only on the evening of 19 May that the weather at last turned favourable. Lindbergh decided to take off in the early morning. That night he was so tense that he could not sleep at all but lay awake for hours, fully aware that every moment of wakefulness reduced his efficiency and thus his chances of success.

At dawn the last preparations were made. Lindbergh intended to take advantage of the prevailing wind across Long Island from the west in daytime but the wind shifted. This meant that he would have to take off not into the wind but with a five-mile-an-hour tail wind.

With the tanks filled up, the plane was holding 145 pounds more than it had ever lifted before in the test flights. To make matters worse, his mechanic told him that owing to the muggy weather his engine was not working at its best. It was forty revolutions low.

Lindbergh had to make a crucial decision. With wind, weather, power and load all unfavourable, his narrow margin of safety was eliminated. Should he take off? He wrote later: "It was then that the intangible elements of flight, experience, intuition, had to take over the final judgement." He was convinced that this was the time to start the flight.

The crowds in the field watched anxiously as the *Spirit of St Louis* gathered speed with agonizing slowness, staggered into the air, fell back and then heaved itself airborne again, clearing the telephone wires by twenty feet, then the trees at the bottom of the field.

Could he do it? This was the question that millions of people both in America and Europe were anxiously asking. He flew with amazing accuracy across Connecticut, Rhode Island, Eastern Massachusetts and Nova Scotia on the route he had set and then headed for Newfoundland.

Once the Newfoundland mountains were behind him it suddenly seemed that sky and sea mirrored each other, for around him there were floating islands of fog and in the sea were white islands too. Icebergs! As the icebergs multiplied so did the fog islands around him. He climbed steadily but the fog climbed with him. At last he came to a wall of cloud so high he could not fly over it and so wide he could not fly round it without great loss of time and fuel. So he plunged into it, flying only by instruments in total darkness. Suddenly he realized that the plane was coated with ice! This was a mortal danger, for ice not only weighed down the plane but could change the curve of the wings and plunge it into the sea.

Fighting down panic he retraced his route to where he had come from and knew the sky to be clear. Finally he burst out of the cloud and headed for Newfoundland again. Then, once more he turned his aircraft towards Europe. From then on he flew round the great thunder-clouds which towered above the floor of cloud, feeling tiny and insignificant amid such mountains.

During the twenty-seventh hour of his flight, he noticed some black specks on the water below him. He was over a fleet of small fishing boats. Circling very low he glimpsed a man's head through a porthole. He closed the throttle and, less than fifty feet away, shouted as loudly as he could:

"Which way is Ireland?"

There was no reply. But during the next hour of his flight he saw land! It was Dingle Bay, Ireland! He was precisely where he had planned to be.

In fact he had accomplished a masterpiece of navigation. In the opinion of his fellow professional pilots, "to have stayed within fifty miles of his course to Ireland would have been luck, to hit it within twenty-five miles would show remarkable navigational ability. To hit it at Dingle Bay was sheer genius."

After Dingle Bay Lindbergh flashed across County Kerry, St George's Channel, Cornwall and the town of Plymouth. (From Plymouth Massachusetts to Plymouth England took less than thirty hours. It had taken the *Mayflower* Pilgrims two months.) It was only after he had turned towards France that he remembered he had had no food since leaving New York so he ate one of the five sandwiches he carried. He no longer counted time in hours. Within minutes the Eiffel Tower and Paris lay below him and at last, from an altitude of 4000 feet, he saw a black square framed by floodlights which, according to his calculations, should be Le Bourget airfield. He circled lower and lower then turned for a straight glide downwards. Finally, very gently, the *Spirit of St Louis'* wheels touched the earth again. After thirty three and a half hours in the air, his historic flight was over.

Two years before the mast

Richard Henry Dana was born in Cambridge, Massachusetts, U.S.A., in 1815. As a young man he settled down to study law until, following an illness, his eyes began to fail. Dana thought that a sea voyage would restore his health, particularly his eyesight. You may think there was nothing very remarkable about that—but Dana's voyage was no luxury cruise. He travelled as a common seaman on a voyage to California to bring back hides. His ship, the *Pilgrim*, sailed from Boston on 14 August 1834. It would be more than two years before Charles Dana would see his home port again.

The *Pilgrim* was a small ship: and her crew numbered only seven men—including a boy aged no more than twelve, Dana and another novice sailor called Stimson, who was soon to become Dana's firm friend.

In command of the men were three officers: a first and second mate, and the Captain himself, Captain Thompson. Thompson was a typical Yankee skipper of the time—tough and a hard driver of ships and men. But for all his aggressiveness, there was something lacking in his seamanship which no amount of driving and bullying could make up for. Somewhat to Dana's surprise, the crew tolerated both the unending work and the severe discipline—for both were common enough on ships of that time.

The *Pilgrim's* course to California took her right down the coast of the North and South American continents (in those days the Panama canal had not been made),

round Cape Horn and all the way up the west coast of South America to California.

In the first stage of the journey, Dana was intent on learning his new, difficult and often highly dangerous job: but it did not take him long to realize the harsh truth about a sailor's life. Death was never very far away, and danger was always present. The first major incident occurred on 19 November.

"All hands ahoy!" went the cry, arousing the watch below at seven in the morning . . . "Man overboard!"

It was George Sallmer, a young English sailor, who had been clambering aloft with a load of equipment when he fell into the sea. He could not swim, and was heavily dressed and loaded. Yet, though all the men

knew he must be lost a boat was launched and rowed around for an hour searching, and hoping.

"Death is always solemn, but never so much so as at sea," wrote Dana. "A dozen men are shut up together in a little bark upon the wide, wide sea, and for months and months see no forms and hear no voices but their own."

The voyage went on, with that much more for the survivors to do, and the *Pilgrim* drove around Cape Horn into the Pacific, towards the nearly deserted coast of early nineteenth-century California.

It was at this time that relations between Captain and crew began seriously to deteriorate. The sailors had so far put up with the ceaseless work, and with being forbidden to speak to each other while doing it. They had put up with endless unravelling of old rope—picking oakum as it was called. They had put up with the appointment of a new third mate when another hand was required to replace George. What finally brought things to a head was a petty dispute involving Dana and his friend Stimson.

These two novice sailors had at first lived in the steerage, the most uncomfortable part of the ship. After four months at sea they were considered to be good enough sailors to move into the fo'c'sle with the other crewmen. Everyone was happy with the new arrangement, but there was a dispute about how much total allowance of bread should now go to the fo'c'sle. It was the kind of dispute that could have been settled in a moment, but not by Captain Thompson. He refused absolutely to explain the situation to his men and was enraged at even being asked.

As if that was not enough, bad news awaited the *Pilgrim* on her arrival in California. Today California is a thriving state: then it was part of Mexico and was very thinly populated. Unfortunately few hides were reaching the coast from the interior, and instead of quickly filling up with cargo

and returning home, the *Pilgrim* had to act as a collecting vessel, shuttling hides from up and down the coast to the central warehouse at San Diego. Worse still, those hides were due to be taken by other ships belonging to the same company, which had to be filled before the *Pilgrim* could collect for herself.

This was a bitter blow, but there was little the men could do. They were bound to their prison. The only way they could get home was to persuade or bribe a crewman on another ship to exchange places with them, but for months no other ships were returning home: for sixteen months the *Pilgrim* sailed to and fro along the Californian coast while the sailors loaded and unloaded thousands of hides.

Discipline on board became even sterner. Part of the trouble was that Mr Amerzene, the mate, was too kindly a man for a ship with a captain like Thompson. The Captain soon became suspicious of his humane methods and came to feel that things were not being done with enough "will". The men were kept permanently at work except when they were asleep and for some little time on Sundays. They worked even when there was nothing really to do, when they were in port and it was raining and the hides could not be loaded. They worked silently, and they worked for hours on end. Almost inevitably, trouble flared again, and this time it was far worse. One of the crewmen was a big, rather slow man, called Sam, hesitant in his speech and "only a tolerably good sailor", though he "usually seemed to do his best." Working in the hold, Sam hurt his hand and began swearing about it, unaware that Captain Thompson was near. The Captain demanded to know what was the matter, but Sam with his speech impediment could not answer very quickly, and when he did, his answer seemed to displease the captain.

"Will you ever give me any more of your jaw?" Thompson demanded. "Will you ever be impudent to me again?"

"I never have been, sir," Sam protested.

"Answer my question, or I'll make a spreadeagle of you! I'll flog you . . ." bellowed the enraged Captain—and in a moment he had ordered Mr Amerzene to seize Sam and spreadeagle him against the rigging, had taken off his coat, and was rolling up his sleeves.

Then another voice broke in. "What are you going to flog that man for, sir?" It was John the Swede. At once the Captain ordered John to be clapped in irons. There was going to be a flogging alright—a double flogging!

Dana's blood ran cold at the savage injustice and cruelty of what he had seen. He vowed then that, somehow, he would do something to redress the grievances and relieve the sufferings of seamen who had to work under brutes like Thompson. Legally, the captain of a ship could do anything he liked with the men under his command and the sailors were kept virtual prisoners on their ships for as long as owners and captains needed them.

As it happened, Dana and his friend Stimson were able to arrange to transfer to another ship the *Alert* and return home. They remained under Captain Thompson nonetheless, for he too transferred, while the former captain of the new ship, Captain Faucon took over on the *Pilgrim*. That at least was a gain for Dana's old shipmates. For Captain Faucon was a finer man than Thompson.

For Dana the way back lay with Thompson, and a bitter journey it proved, with a tremendous battle to round Cape Horn in the teeth of the very worst storms of the year. For days and nights the men worked soaked to the skin in freezing weather, while the *Alert* dodged icebergs and huge seas swept the ship's deck. But the discomforts of the voyage were not charged equally. Captain Thompson was not neglectful of his duty—he spent long hours on deck as they battled through the storms—but he cared nothing for the welfare of his men.

He saw to it that his steward brought him a regular supply of hot drinks, but never once did he do the same for his half-frozen sailors. The *Alert* carried a number of live animals for food (pigs, sheep, poultry) but hardly any fresh meat reached the crew, and though salt beef was the basic diet of everyone on board, the Captain's steward selected all the best for "the cabin", leaving tough, dry meat for the crew.

After four months at sea on the return journey, scurvy broke out among the men. Scurvy was for a long time a great danger to sailors on long voyages, but by Dana's time everyone knew it was caused by the lack of fresh food—chiefly vegetables which contain vitamin C and many ships carried supplies of lime juice for this very reason. The *Alert* did not and young Ben, an English sailor in the crew, came within a week of death, before being saved by a lucky accident. The *Alert* happened to pass another ship carrying a cargo of fresh vegetables, and the boatload of potatoes and onions that was hastily rowed across from one ship to the other saved Ben's life—and probably prevented more cases of scurvy occurring.

Of course, the crew found the hardships of the return journey easier to bear because they knew they were going home. After the storms of the Cape were passed the voyage did have its pleasant side and Dana had time to notice "the sails shining like white marble in the moonlight of a starry tropical night, while the warm trade winds breathed steadily from astern". And there was this, too, about Dana's journey, which ended 137 days after they left California: it had made him magnificently healthy and so restored his eyesight that he was soon able to resume his studies and follow a successful career in law.

Though Dana succeeded as a lawyer, his real fame rests on his journey: for the book he wrote about his experiences, *Two Years Before the Mast*, is a unique document in the history of the sea.

A South American journey

In the early nineteenth century, Spain had many colonies in South America. Most of the Spanish settlements were along the coast, for little was known about the centre of the continent, which was believed to be a region of mystery and danger.

One of the first people to explore far inland was the geologist Alexander von Humboldt. Von Humboldt was born in Berlin in 1769. Before he set off on the expedition he had become a friend of Aimé Bonpland, a young French botanist. They made a strange pair: von Humboldt over six feet in height and Bonpland small and frail-looking. They worked out a plan to explore the Orinoco river and its tributaries, a network of rivers stretching for over 1500 miles across northern South America. They hoped to find the source of the great river whose estuary Columbus had discovered and to make a study of the rocks, plants and animals of the country. To do this they had

to get a permit from the Spanish King and in May 1799 they left Madrid on foot for Corunna where they boarded a packet boat for Cuba. They arrived at Cumana in Venezuela on 16 July.

For about six months they spent their time exploring the coast. Bonpland found many unusual plants and flowers and von Humboldt made maps and studied the weather and the tides.

Everywhere von Humboldt went he took with him large amounts of scientific equipment. (The Spanish authorities had supplied porters and mules to help carry all the tents and stores.) At night von Humboldt and Bonpland would sit in their tent studying their latest discoveries. All the specimens of plants and insects were carefully examined and then stored.

Von Humboldt described the way the Indians hunted the electric eels that lived in the marshy regions. They would surround a marsh and drive mules and horses into the water to disturb the eels with long poles of bamboo. The sudden rush of the animals frightened the eels and caused them to let off charges of electricity. "Gradually the fury of the unequal struggle begins to slacken," wrote von Humboldt. "Like clouds which have discharged their electricity, the wearied fish scatter. . . . their shocks become weaker and weaker. Terrified by the noise of the trampling horses, they timidly approach the bank where they are wounded by harpoons and cautiously drawn on shore by non-conducting pieces of dry wood."

On 26 March 1800 von Humboldt and Bonpland arrived at the banks of the River Apure, a tributary of the great Orinoco. They had had a hard journey, cutting their way through dense jungles. With four Indian rowers and a pilot to guide them, they set off in a small sailing canoe with a cabin roofed with leaves.

The river was two miles wide at this point and they were making slow but steady progress in their frail canoe when a sudden squall of wind snatched at them and knocked them off course. Before they knew what was happening, the boat had tilted over and water was beginning to flood in. The river was full of alligators but some of the Indians started to swim towards the bank. Bonpland could not swim but he shouted to von Humboldt to save himself if he could. There seemed little hope for any of them. The river banks were choked with dense jungle and even if they could escape the alligators and the currents, there was little hope of surviving for long in such a wild country. Then, just as suddenly, another strong gust of wind blew the canoe upright again and they were saved!

Soon they reached the Orinoco river itself and began their journey upstream. As well as collecting specimens of plants and animals, they hoped to find the source of the Orinoco and to trace an inland waterway, the Casiquiari Canal, which was thought to link the Orinoco to the Amazon river. They sailed up the Orinoco for thirty-six days, avoiding cataracts and rapids where they could, before they reached the Casiquiari.

Day after day they suffered from the great heat, from the bites of thousands of insects and from the dangers of the river itself with its rapids and waterfalls. When they at last reached the tributaries of the Amazon, von Humboldt wrote: "After all we had endured, I may be permitted, perhaps, to speak of the the satisfaction we felt in having reached the tributary streams of the Amazon, having passed the isthmus that separates two great systems of rivers, and in being sure of having fulfilled the most important object of our voyage, the astronomical determination of the course of that arm of the Orinoco, which falls in the Rio Negro and of which the existence has been alternately proved and denied for half a century."

Everywhere there were forests, but there was no sign of human beings. Animals were all around them: alligators and strange fish in the rivers, monkeys and brightly-coloured birds in the forests. Their boat was by this time like a floating zoo. They had seven parrots, eight monkeys, one dog, a macaw and a toucan. Von Humboldt wrote a lot about what he saw but he was also a talented artist and he filled his notebooks with beautifully coloured pictures of animals, plants and scenery.

Having discovered that the Casiquiari was a natural canal about two hundred miles long, they travelled back along it to the Orinoco. Then they went eastwards to a small settlement called Esmeralda, which was used as a penal colony. Here they heard tales about the source of the Orinoco but, fearing attacks from hostile Indians, they did not venture any further upstream. In fact the source of the Orinoco was not finally established until 1951.

Their next South American journey took them across the Andes to Lima in Peru. It was not an easy journey. They set off up the Magdalene river, fighting all the time against dangerously rapid currents. Then they had to shelter from terrible gales and raging thunderstorms. It took them forty-five days to cover three hundred miles. News of their approach to Bogota had gone ahead of them and they were welcomed as highly important visitors. The archbishop sent his carriage to meet them and they entered the town in a grand procession. Bells were rung and trumpets sounded from the tops of buildings, while women leaned from the windows of houses to throw flowers into the carriage.

From Bogota they went on to the town of Quito and then spent their time exploring the nearby hills and volcanoes. At the end of May von Humboldt climbed a volcano called Pichincha. He wrote: "The first journey I made alone with an Indian. Since Condamine had approached the crater from the snow covered side of the rim, I followed in his footsteps. That was nearly the end of us. The Indian sank up to his chest in a crevasse and we discovered to our horror that we had passed over a bridge of iced snow. A few steps away we could see daylight. Without realizing it, we had stood on vaults overlooking the crater."

Von Humboldt lay flat on a rock which stuck out like a balcony. He could look down at the bottom of the crater, and as he did so the rock trembled from the rumblings of the volcano. Dense sulphur fumes nearly suffocated them as they watched the bluish flames flickering below. Humboldt and the Indian managed to reach safety and in spite of the dangers he had faced, he was determined to climb even higher. On 9 June 1802 von Humboldt and Bonpland began what was to be a record-breaking climb of Mount Chimborazo.

For this climb von Humboldt and Bonpland travelled on foot with porters and oxen carrying their baggage. They reached a plateau at about 10,000 feet where there was still plant life, but as they climbed higher there was only bare rock, and finally snow. With nearly 3000 feet still to go to the summit, the porters became frightened and refused to climb any higher. For another 2000 feet Humboldt and Bonpland struggled on alone until they came to a great crack in the rock which it was impossible to cross. Here they took the air pressure and made scientific notes. They had reached 18,440 feet, a world record which was to stand for nearly thirty years.

Both Bonpland and von Humboldt wrote books about their discoveries and travels. Bonpland returned to South America as a Professor of Natural History. Von Humboldt still had long journeys to make in Siberia. His greatest book, called *Cosmos*, was written when he was over seventy. It sets out everything that was known at that time about the stars, the earth and the oceans. The dangers and hardships of travel seem not to have harmed his health for, unlike other nineteenth century travellers, he lived to a great age: he died on 6 May 1859 at the age of ninety.

The Kon Tiki

Thor Heyerdahl is a Norwegian scientist who once spent some time studying plant and animal life on the small Pacific island of Fatuhiva. While he was there, a strange theory began to form in his mind. He noticed that the people of Polynesia, scattered over hundreds of islands and thousands of square miles, all spoke dialects of the same language. He also noticed a strange similarity between the stone figures of the Polynesian god Tiki on Fatuhiva, the unexplained stone heads on Easter island two thousand miles to the east, and the mysterious pre-Inca statues found in Peru. What could the connection be?

The Polynesian people themselves had light-coloured skin, blue-grey eyes, hooked noses and reddish hair. They claimed descent from the original rulers of the islands, and told Heyerdahl that their ancestors had come from a mountainous land across the sea to the east. Heyerdahl already knew that the islands were first populated around 500 A.D. by a stoneage people of an advanced culture and he now realized that a migration like this could only have come from South America. After more study he came to the conclusion that the first people to live on

these Pacific islands must have migrated from Peru.

In Peru there were legends of a white race which had taught the Incas their science and art, but whose leader had been defeated in battle and had fled across the sea. The name of the leader had been Kon Tiki, surely the same god that had once been worshipped in Polynesia. Kon Tiki's people had not been shipbuilders, but it was known that they used rafts made of balsa wood, lashed together with ropes, held steady by centreboards and steered by a single oar.

On 28 April 1947, Thor Heyerdahl and five companions set out from Callao in Peru bound for Polynesia. They built a careful

reconstruction of the kind of raft the pre-Inca people must have used. What they were trying to do was to act out what had happened in history, to show what they thought had *probably* happened 1400 years before. If they succeeded, then Heyerdahl's theory would at least be acceptable as a possible explanation; if they failed, if the raft broke up or became water-logged, as every expert predicted, then the theory would be dismissed and they would all be killed.

They named the raft *Kon Tiki* after the great god who was ancestor god to the Polynesians and god of fire and sun for pre-Inca Peruvians. The *Kon Tiki* was heavy and floated low in the water because the balsa logs she was made of were still full of sap; dry logs would have become water-logged very quickly. The logs were lashed together with ropes. Steering was done with a single oar of pine wood and pine centreboards let down between the nine main logs. She was just eighteen feet wide and forty-five feet long. There was no engine. The only sign of modern life was a medical kit, a rubber dinghy and a tiny transmitter.

Although the travellers carried provisions for a hundred days they intended to live off what they could catch from the sea.

Among the six travellers only one, Eric Hasselberg, had any experience of the sea. He was working as an artist in ordinary life but now became navigator. Of the others, Heyerdahl was a scientist as was Bengt Danielsson; Herman Watzinger was an engineer, and Knut Haugland and Torstein Raaby were radio specialists. All were Norwegian, except Bengt, who was Swedish.

For the first sixty hours the voyage seemed as bad as the pessimists had predicted. The seas in the cold Humboldt Current were high, the raft exhausting to control. The ropes seemed to be chafing and rubbing badly, and worst of all, the high wind drove them in the wrong direction.

Gradually the wind veered round and their confidence grew as they acquired the knack of using the centreboards to hold a course. They were soon sailing through the blue, sedately-rolling waters of the open Pacific. Flying fish became increasingly common, providing not only excellent breakfasts but also bait for catching other fish.

The Pacific proved rich in fish of all kinds and sizes, from tiny plankton (which they collected in a net and ate), to tunny, dolphins, sharks and whales.

On 24 May the raft had a dramatic encounter with the biggest fish of all. Knut saw it first. He was doing some washing in the stern when he glanced up to find himself face to face, at a range of a few feet, with the biggest, ugliest creature he had ever seen. Its face was flat like a frog's, with two small eyes at the sides and an enormously wide, flat mouth with long fringes at the corners. It was brownish in colour and covered with white spots; it had a pointed tail and a large dorsal fin. It was a shark — a whale shark. These can grow to sixty-five feet long and weigh fifteen tons. If this one wasn't quite that big, it was certainly bigger than the raft, which it could have smashed to pieces with just a casual flick of its tail. Instead it just circled stupidly, getting closer and closer, while the minutes passed and tension rose.

At last, Erik could stand the huge ugly island of muscle no longer and he thrust a harpoon into it. Next moment the monster crash dived, leaving behind the school of pilot fish which had been swimming in front of its nose (they promptly adopted *Kon Tiki* as a new 'shark' to guide), a sheet of oil on the water and a bent harpoon. For most of the four thousand mile journey they had perfect weather. But on 16 June a storm blew up and *Kon Tiki* was soon riding fifteen foot high waves.

In the course of the next twenty-four hours Heyerdahl calculated that the raft probably shipped ten thousand tons of water but for all that it continued to ride the sea like some great balsa steamroller: for no sooner had the stern disappeared under a breaking wave, than the water ran off through the logs, the bow lifted and she was clear again.

After the storm had lasted a day there was a short pause; then it began again, with redoubled fury. This time it lasted three days —and left *Kon Tiki* heavily damaged. The massive steering oar was smashed, the sail ripped, the centreboards loosened and made virtually useless. All this damage was quickly repaired, however—all except the centreboards which could not be completely restored. They would soon be missed.

By the end of July the last lap of the journey was fast approaching. On the 30th they sighted land. It was Puka-Puka, most northerly outpost of the Tuamotu group. Within an hour they were close enough to smell the forest. At the same time they discovered that without the full use of their centreboards they could not steer *Kon Tiki* out of the eye of the wind. Regretfully they watched Puka-Puka drop astern. They had certainly reached Polynesia. The problem now was whether they would be able to land.

Three days later the same wind that had blown them past Puka-Puka and later past the island of Angatau blew them directly at a third island—and no-one could have chosen a more dangerous place. They found that *Kon Tiki* was heading straight for the notorious Raroia barrier reef. This is fifty miles long and more than a hundred yards wide. Its edges are jagged and it is pounded by mountainous breakers.

Calmly, everything was lashed down. The centreboards were brought right up to help the raft float over the "step" of the reef and, as they drifted sideways towards the island, an improvised sea-anchor of empty cans and logs was trailed behind on a rope. In the cabin the radio operators kept up a constant flow of transmissions to radio stations all over the world, describing their approach and giving their position.

Anxiously they tried to find a gap in the reef but *Kon Tiki* was beyond their control and was making straight for the reef of Takume, last but one of the islands in the group. The steering oar was abandoned, for steering was impossible and the stern of the raft was the most dangerous place to be. The sea anchor grounded and corrected their sideways drift and was then cut clear. Then they clung on for their lives as *Kon Tiki* carried along by the huge waves, charged the wall of the reef. As they rose high in the air it seemed possible that they would hurtle across at the first attempt.

But no. The wave spent itself and the raft fell back among the eddies at the foot of the reef step. At the same moment another wave rose up like a solid green glass wall. Up and up it climbed, higher than the mast, then down it smashed against the raft, threatening to suck all the travellers from where they were clinging, into the deadly surf.

Again and again the raft was battered by huge seas and yet miraculously, no damage was done. Then a fourth wave—the biggest so far—came rolling in. This time the raft was flung bodily at the reef wall. *Kon Tiki* took a terrible battering. The massive steering oar was shattered to matchwood. The great mangrove wood mast was broken, the deck torn, the cabin flattened.

They were pinned to the reef by the force of the sea—caught between the hammer of the waves and the anvil of the coral. Time and again the nearly-solid walls of water crashed down on them. Then all at once Heyerdahl and his companions realized that the power of the waves had diminished, that only the tops were breaking over them.

Ahead lay the bright white sand of the island and the lagoon. They had done it!

Kon Tiki was perched on top of the reef and every wave moved her further in. Though they had been badly battered they were still in one piece: like her ancestors, *Kon Tiki* had carried men safely across four thousand miles of sea, and nothing the wind, or the Pacific or coral reefs could do had been able to stop her.

The lake that disappears

The coast of West Africa has been known to travellers and traders from Europe since the fifteenth century. Inland, however, little was known about either the country or the people who lived there until much later. Protected in the north by the great Sahara desert, and in the west by unexplored rainforest, the fabulous city of Timbuktu and the mysterious Lake Chad were known only from the tales of merchants trading with the Tuareg nomads. Early in the nineteenth century two white men managed to visit Timbuktu: Major Gordon Laing, in 1826 and Réné Caillié in 1828. Major Laing was killed there but Réné Caillié, disguised as an Arab trader, managed to stay there long enough to observe the city and its people and to learn about its civilization.

Heinrich Barth was lecturing in geography at Berlin university when, in 1847, he joined the first scientific expedition across the Sahara to Central Africa and Lake Chad. He had studied Arabic and had already travelled in North Africa and, although he had been attacked and wounded on his last expedition, he was eager to go

again. The leader of the expedition was James Richardson, a British explorer who had already crossed the Sahara and now wanted to reach Lake Chad. The third member was Adolf Overweg, a geologist and astronomer.

Richardson, Barth and Overweg left Tripoli in March 1850 with a caravan of sixty-two camels carrying goods to trade with, and the two halves of a boat which was to be assembled when they reached Lake Chad. They travelled south to Murzuq where they had to wait for a month while local chiefs arranged for them to have a Tuareg escort. By the middle of June they were moving westwards towards Ghat.

The desert stretched before them: hundreds of miles of hot, dry wilderness, of shifting sand dunes and barren rocks. During the day the hot sun glared down at them and at night the clear, cold sky was full of stars. There were no roads in those days, only the ancient Arab tracks from oasis to oasis. Without their Tuareg guides, who spent their lives in the desert, their caravan would soon have been hopelessly lost.

It was at this stage of the journey that Barth nearly lost his life. He was always fond of wandering off on his own and his curiosity was roused by hearing the Tuareg talk of a mountain they claimed was bewitched. In spite of the great heat, Barth set off alone with some dry biscuits, dates and water carried in a skin, in an attempt to reach the top of the high hill of sand. He had to walk on sharp pointed stones and the distance was much greater than he had at first imagined. To reach the summit he had first to descend into a ravine and then climb up the other side. When at last he scrambled to the top he was exposed to the full power of the sun.

He descended into the ravine again and drank the water left in the skin. Soon he was quite lost. He fired his pistols in a vain effort to attract attention, but no one came and, too exhausted to go any farther, he resigned himself to spending the night on the hillside. By noon the next day he was still lost and, half delirious with thirst, he deliberately wounded himself, and moistened his cracked lips with his own blood. Then he collapsed. Fortunately a Tuareg on his camel found him lying unconscious and helped him back to camp.

They had passed Ghat and were around half-way across the desert when their Tuareg guides suddenly turned against them. The Tuaregs were Moslems and they threatened to kill the white men if they would not change their religion. The three travellers sat in their tent, helplessly waiting to die. But for some reason—perhaps because they were armed—the expected attack did not come and they continued their journey. This was not the only time their lives were threatened. As they crossed the Air Mountains, a band of Tuareg robbers came at them suddenly, catching them quite unprepared. Before they had a chance to resist they were surrounded and the caravan was captured. At first the bandits wanted to kill them but they eventually allowed them to go free—in return for a large part of their stores.

On 10 January they reached Tagelel and decided that the expedition should divide into three groups. Barth was to go to Kano and then meet Richardson at Kukawa in Bornu. Barth and Overweg were to stay together for some of the way. They all agreed to meet again at Lake Chad. By February Barth had arrived in the walled city of Kano. He found that he had to give presents to the ruler before he was allowed to go out in the streets but after ten months in the desert it must have been a relief to be among people and houses again and to sleep in a room instead of a tent.

Soon it was time for Barth to make his way to Lake Chad to meet Richardson and Overweg. He travelled first along the banks of the river Yobe to Kukawa where he had planned to meet Richardson. But when he got there he found that Richardson had died three weeks before. Barth recovered his notes and personal belongings and sent them back to Tripoli with a trading caravan that was going that way. Then he went on to Lake Chad.

The great lake had first been written about by the Egyptian geographer Ptolemy in the second century A.D. It was described again in the middle ages, but few Europeans had visited it before Barth and Overweg. Lying on the borders of modern Nigeria, Cameroun, Niger and Chad, it is probably the remains of a great inland sea which existed in prehistoric times. In the north it is held in by high sand dunes, but in the south it becomes shallow and swampy. In wet seasons it fills up with water but in the dry season the water evaporates rapidly and it turns into a vast swamp; covered with islands of reeds and vegetation.

The boat which had been carried so many thousands of miles across the desert was now reassembled and Overweg set about the task of exploring Lake Chad while Barth investigated the arid region round it. Then, leaving his camp he went south to explore the River Benue which flowed into the Niger. With three camels and five horses carrying supplies for his expedition, crossing the river was a problem. It was impossible to put the animals in a canoe, and the water was too deep to wade, so they had to be persuaded to swim. The camels were especially difficult. Animals of the desert, they were quite unused to deep water and would only go in after a great deal of pushing, shouting and beating with sticks. The man who owned the canoe which carried the supplies took full advantage of the situation and made Barth pay the equivalent of the cost of two oxen loads of corn.

There was a sudden tragedy when Barth returned. Overweg had been ill with fever when Barth had met him before his expedition to the Benue river. Since then he had had constant attacks of fever and one day he collapsed and died by the banks of the lake. Barth was now alone, the sole survivor of the expedition. He had already completed a vast programme of exploration but instead of now returning to Tripoli and safety, he decided to go westwards to the famous city of Timbuktu. Ten months later he was outside the walls of the city which only two Europeans had seen.

He stayed at the home of a man called Sheikh el Bakhai, and, remembering what had happened to Major Laing, he decided it would be safest to disguise himself as an Arab.

Timbuktu was a disappointment to Barth. He had heard so much about this great trading centre, with its markets for salt and gold, but he found it a place of great heat and squalor. The long, exhausting journey had made him ill and, to add to his difficulties, the local people soon saw through his disguise. They were hostile and once when he was out with El Bakhai they were surrounded by a mob. Barth dispersed them by firing his revolver into the air, but it was a dangerous moment. For six months Barth stayed either in the house or in a camp outside the city, prevented by illness and fear of attack from exploring as much as he would have liked.

In May 1854 he set out once more with a Tuareg caravan. He travelled down the river Niger to a place called Say, then back to Kano and Bornu. There, to his surprise, he found a rescue party waiting for him — and he was delighted to see them. He had explored a vast region between Lake Chad and Timbuktu (he covered 10,000 miles in all) and was now ready to return home. He had been away for nearly six years.

On his return he was honoured in both Germany and England for his achievements and discoveries. When he died, at the age of forty-four, from an illness he had first caught in Africa, he left behind a wealth of written information that was of great value to the explorers who followed him.

Round the world in eighty days

This is the story of an imaginary journey, written by the Frenchman, Jules Verne, at the end of the last century. It is about an Englishman who is mad enough to bet £20,000 that he can travel round the world in eighty days. You must remember that at the time of this story there were no aeroplanes, ships were run by steam, and there were very few cars. The methods of travel used on the journey had to be those available at the time in whichever country the hero found himself. As it turned out, he used steamers, railways, carriages, yachts, merchant ships, a wind sledge and an elephant.

The very English hero is *Phileas Fogg* who employs a very French servant, called *Passepartout*. (This means literally "the man-who-can-get-out-of-anything".) Trailing along behind them is a detective called *Fix*. He thinks Phileas Fogg has robbed the Bank of England and is trying to arrest him. The other person you will meet is a beautiful Indian girl called Aouda who joins the party in dramatic circumstances.

One day Mr Phileas Fogg was sitting in his club playing cards, according to his daily habit, when there was an unusual stir. It turned out that the Bank of England had been robbed and the thief had escaped! Members of the club were laying bets as to how far the thief could get in how short a time. Someone remarked that the thief *could* get all round the world in eighty days. He read out the details from the newspaper, but no-one really believed it was possible: so Phileas' enormous bet of £20,000 was

accepted, and the adventure began. In eighty days time, before 8.45 in the evening, they must have completed their journey round the world . . .

The first lap of the journey was from London to Bombay, via Suez. Thanks to a bribe which Phileas Fogg gave to the Captain of the steam ship from Suez, he was able to put "two days" under the heading GAINS in the notebook where he was keeping a record.

Little did they know, however, that their troubles were beginning. A certain detective attached to the Metropolitan Police, called Fix, had noticed Phileas Fogg when the ship docked at Suez. He was one of the plain-clothes men on the look-out for the Bank of England robber. Phileas Fogg seemed to match exactly the description which had been circulated. Full of excitement (there was a reward for the man who arrested the robber) Fix sent off for a warrant to arrest him. Meanwhile he resolved to keep an eye on the two men by being friendly with Passepartout.

The train from Bombay to Calcutta started at eight in the evening. Phileas Fogg, Passepartout, and Fix were among the passengers. Unfortunately the railway line finished before they reached Calcutta. Everyone else knew this and had taken every available means of transport before Phileas Fogg knew what was happening. He was quite unworried, however, and with Passepartout began to look for a suitable vehicle. It was Passepartout who found what they needed: an elephant belonging to a man who was training it to fight in wars. After some discussion between Phileas Fogg and the owner, the elephant became the property of Phileas Fogg. They thought it best to hire an Indian boy as well, who could understand it.

Phileas Fogg was given a kind of saddle called a *howdah* to sit on, but Passepartout had to bounce about on the elephant's back. The boy rode on its neck. They trotted along

for a day and spent one night camping. The next evening they were going along when they heard weird cries and music. Hiding in the bushes, they saw a long procession of Indian priests and people pass by. Most important among them seemed to be a young-ish girl who was staggering along led by the priests, and a large stretcher, on which lay the dead body of an old man, covered in jewels. The boy explained to the others that the girl had been the old man's wife and that now he had died his body was to be burned. According to this Indian religion, the girl had to be burned as well—to keep him company in the next life.

Phileas Fogg was thinking hard. By this time he had lost some of the time gained at Bombay but he still had a day in hand. He decided in his usual cool way that they must wait and rescue the girl.

In the morning Phileas Fogg and the guide stood with the crowd as the fire was lit. Suddenly the old man on the stretcher sat up! The crowd was horrified and thrown into complete confusion. Phileas Fogg of course kept his head. Sure enough the "old man", now looking increasingly like Passepartout, came running towards them, dragging the girl with him. There was no time for explanations; they all scrambled onto the elephant and made off into the jungle. As they went, shots rang out around them and they knew that their trick had been discovered.

The girl was Aouda. When she had recovered she told them that she had had an entirely European education but when she returned to India she had been forced to marry the old man. In spite of one attempt to escape she had been unable to get far enough away from her ex-husband's family, who were determined that she should die. Now of course she was very grateful to Passepartout who had taken the place of the old man's body and rescued her.

They reached the station where they could catch a train for Calcutta and Phileas Fogg gave the worthy elephant to their

Indian guide as a reward for all his help.

All this time Fix had been close behind them. He wanted to arrest Phileas Fogg before he reached America where his warrant would be useless. When they reached Calcutta he followed them on the steamer to Hong Kong and by various crafty methods managed to make Phileas Fogg lose Passepartout and miss the steamer for Japan. It was vital for Phileas Fogg to reach Japan in time to catch the steamer for San Francisco, and, unworried as usual, he managed to hire a very small boat with a Captain who would take him, Aouda and Fix on the way to Japan.

They eventually arrived there just in time to find Passepartout and to catch a schooner for America.

At San Francisco they caught a train which was to take them 3,786 miles across America to New York. The journey would take them across wild, bare country, and only Phileas Fogg seemed confident that all would go well. The first trouble came when they heard that the train was approaching a rather unsafe bridge, crossing a very steep gorge. It was decided to rush the bridge by making the train go at full speed so that it would be forced across before the bridge collapsed. Once decided, this was what they did: the engine driver reversed the train a little way, built up an enormous head of steam and started off at a speed of nearly one hundred miles per hour. Everything happened in a flash. The train roared across the bridge just a few seconds before the whole thing collapsed. Phileas Fogg continued calmly playing cards.

More trouble was to follow when the train was attacked by Sioux Indians, and when they finally arrived at the docks of New York, the Liverpool steamer had left less than an hour before.

Mr Phileas Fogg of course took this in his stride. With some difficulty he found a boat which would take them, but they only reached Liverpool after Phileas Fogg had locked up the Captain and taken over the ship! He did give it back to the Captain however, with a lot of money, when they reached the port.

So Phileas Fogg, Aouda and Passepartout found themselves at Liverpool all ready to make a last dash for London to claim the £20,000.

It was at this point that Fix made his move. Just as Phileas Fogg was stepping onto the train for London, he heard the words "I arrest you in the Queen's name," and felt the heavy hand of Fix on his shoulder.

Precious hours were wasted at the police station before it was found that Fix had been wrong all the time. The real robber had been caught three days before!

It was 2.0 p.m. when they left and they were now running very short of time indeed. Phileas Fogg went straight to the station and chartered a train for London. When they reached the London station all the clocks said ten to nine. All their efforts had been in vain: they were five minutes late. It seemed as though Phileas Fogg had not only lost his bet but spent all his money as well.

At home again, the only happy part about the whole thing was that Phileas Fogg and Aouda decided to get married the day after they arrived. Passepartout was sent to arrange things. Suldenly he reappeared. He found that because they had crossed the international date-line during the journey, they had actually saved a whole day. Today, not yesterday was the day when they were due at the Club.

Without another word, they all rushed out of the house, bought the nearest vehicle, and made all possible speed to the meeting place. Exactly one second before he was due, in came Phileas Fogg. He had won back his cheque for £20,000, found a wife and was thoroughly contented—exactly as he had always intended.

The way to the north

Settlers began to arrive in Australia towards the end of the eighteenth century. They chose the most favourable farming country that had been discovered, in south Australia, near where Sydney is today. The first explorers who ventured beyond the Blue Mountains reported that there was good grass there for those who dared to make the journey. But what lay beyond this? What lay in the centre of Australia?

John McDouall Stuart was already an experienced map-maker and surveyor when he went with Charles Sturt on a journey to find the centre of Australia in 1844. Charles Sturt had come to Australia as a captain in the British army in 1826, in charge of a group of convicts. Two years later he led an expedition to the interior of Australia and discovered the Darling River. On later

journeys he found the Murrumbidgee and the Murray rivers but still he wanted to go further.

"I have a strange idea," he wrote, "that there may be a central sea not far from the Darling."

Apart from Sturt and Stuart there were fourteen other men in the party, with eleven horses, thirty bulls and two hundred sheep. They also took with them a boat—to use on the sea they hoped to find.

They reached the Barrier Range and a creek which Sturt named after his friend Charles Cooper, a lawyer who later became the Chief Justice of Australia. Now they experienced terrible heat and because they could not find fresh fruit to eat they developed scurvy. But they found no inland sea, and no fertile pasture for their sheep

and bulls. In October 1845 they reached a stony desert and after Sturt, Stuart and two other men had explored a little further to the north, they decided to return.

The journey back to Adelaide took them over two months. By the time they arrived, in January 1846, Sturt had been temporarily blinded by the constant glare of the sun.

Stuart was brave, careful and very determined in everything he did. Though with Sturt he had failed to reach the centre of Australia, he felt sure that this could eventually be done. He also believed that it must be possible to travel overland from the south to the north, a distance of about 1700 miles. In 1858 and 1859 he explored the regions around Lake Torens and Mount Fincke in preparation for an attempt, and when, in 1859, the South Australian government offered a £2000 reward to the first man to cross from south to north, Stuart was ready to try again.

Stuart took only two other men and thirteen horses on his journey to the north. They went through country that had never been explored before. Some of the regions they passed Stuart believed would one day be fine country for sheep and cattle farmers. Then they came to vast, prairie-like lands where great rocks rose up to make weird shapes against the landscape. Gradually the grass grew more sparsely, and was replaced by spiky spinifex plants. They had to use all their water supply for themselves and for two days their horses had none at all.

At last they reached the mountain that is now called Mount Freeling and found water nearby. Sixteen years before, Sturt and Stuart had failed to reach the centre of Australia. This time, on 22 April 1860, Stuart calculated that he was there at last. He piled up some stones and set up the Union Jack at a place that was later called Central Mount Stuart after him.

They explored first to the east and then travelled north again, but they found the local people unfriendly. After being attacked by the Aborigines with boomerangs, Stuart decided that the expedition had gone far enough and so they turned and headed south, back to Adelaide.

Though Stuart's reports about the interior were not all promising, the government still believed that if an overland route could be found to the north, great trading benefits would follow. For this reason they agreed to pay for the equipment Stuart needed to lead a new expedition. While plans for this were going ahead there was great excitement in Melbourne. Two more travellers, Robert O'Hara Burke and William Wills, had raised £9000 to finance a rival expedition to the north. Large crowds turned out to cheer as Burke, mounted on a camel, led his party out of town. The newspapers called it the "Great Australian Exploration Race".

Even before Stuart left Adelaide, Wills and Burke were in difficulties and in fact their expedition ended in disaster. They did reach the northern coast, but on the return journey only one man survived, John King. The twenty-seven camels that had been specially imported from India for the journey were abandoned—and their descendants today live wild in the central desert.

When Stuart left Adelaide at the beginning of 1861 with a small party, he knew very well the terrible risks that they were taking.

They journeyed north as far as the place now called Newcastle Waters, less than six hundred miles from the northern coast. Stuart had hoped to find fertile land but instead there was nothing but dry scrubland with no sign of water. He decided not to risk the lives of his men and returned to Adelaide to rest and re-equip.

By 26 October, Stuart and his party of seven were ready to set off again. Retracing their steps through the hilly country north of Adelaide, past the salt lakes, they reached the scrubland and semi-deserts: by April 1862 they were once more at Newcastle Waters. This time they managed to find water holes, but it needed great determination to keep going. On 6 June Stuart wrote in his diary:

"After passing over a rotten plain full of holes and covered with grass and stunted gum trees, proceeded to the top where we had a good view of the surrounding countryside: to all appearances one of the blackest and most dismal views a man ever beheld."

A few people managed to live in this harsh country. Once more Aborigines appeared and the little party prepared to defend themselves. Fortunately the Aborigines were friendly, although they seemed very frightened of the horses—especially when one showed its teeth.

Further north the scenery changed again. They passed through beautiful mountain valleys with dense forests. All around were strange sights, including birds and plants that they had never seen before.

The horses were now desperately tired. In the stony desert they had crossed earlier the ground had been so hard and dry that the horses had begun to be lame as their shoes wore out. Now, when they were near the end of the journey the dry grass stuck to their legs, hampering them as they made their way up the hills. But Stuart was confident. They had passed the Roper River and now came to a wide, slow-moving river they named the Adelaide. Here there was no longer any dry grass to trouble them and after so many months of heat and dust it was marvellous to see water lilies floating on the river and flocks of waterbirds—including pelicans—swimming and fishing in the water.

As they reached tropical palm groves they were constantly pestered by mosquitoes but by now they were too excited to care. On 24 July they turned due north and Stuart heard at last what he had been waiting for—the sound of the sea. Sure enough as they forced their way through the thick undergrowth one of the party suddenly shouted:

"The sea! The sea!"

Tired though they were they summoned up enough strength to rush forward to get their first glimpse of the ocean. It was a great moment for them. All the months of hard travel now seemed worthwhile. Stuart climbed to the top of the highest tree he could find and after tying a Union Jack to its branches he shouted to his men to give three cheers. They cheered as loudly as their dry throats would allow them!

They spent only one day resting by the sea before setting off again on the long homeward journey. It was to be even harder than the journey north. Burke and Wills had died during their return journey and as Stuart and his men moved south they noticed with horror that many of the lakes and ponds they were relying on for water were drying up. The intense heat and the lack of rain made water desperately short. As they reached the scrubland there was no sign of life and therefore no opportunity to hunt and catch food.

The horses had served them well but the short rest at the ocean had not been enough for them. They soon became lame again when they reached the hard, stony desert region and they always needed water. Some, worn out and exhausted, died before they reached new water supplies. Stuart rested his party at every opportunity for they were now ill with scurvy and half starved. Stuart himself was so ill that he could no longer walk and had to be carried on a stretcher slung between two of the surviving horses. He had lost the use of his right hand and his eyes were so affected by the constant glare of the sun that he was almost blind. Slowly they made their way to the south.

At last they began to see familiar country that reminded them of home and on 18 December they finally reached Adelaide.

Eight years later Stuart's journey was proved to have found the most direct route to the north: the overland telegraph from Port Augusta to Darwin was laid almost exactly along the way he had pioneered.

Lost on the ice

Fridtjof Nansen was born in 1861 on the outskirts of Christiania (now Oslo), in Norway. He was a man of many talents and considerable energy. Although he is remembered now as a courageous and imaginative explorer, he was also a scientist, an artist, and, in later years, a statesman who won the Nobel Peace Prize in 1922.

As a young man, Nansen was an enthusiastic athlete, a keen hunter and fisherman, and, like so many Norwegians, a natural skier and skater. In fact, Nansen's fondness for outdoor life, together with his dedication to science, led to his choice of zoology as the subject he decided to study at university. It was also essentially this combination of intellectual interest and physical skill which was to make him so effective as a scientist, an explorer, and not least, a survivor.

Nansen's first experience of Arctic conditions came early in his life. He had joined the whaling ship, *Viking* which was travelling between Spitzbergen and Greenland as a geological observer. It was the sight of the vast Greenland ice-cap which first fired his imagination. Later, "the great adventure of the ice", its scientific study, the strangeness and beauty of the frozen Arctic world, were all to be recorded by him.

It was the ice-cap of Greenland which provided Nansen with his first serious ex-pedition. In 1888 he decided not only that he would cross it, when others had failed before him, but that he would do so on skis and sledges. Apart from the fact that the party of six which eventually crossed the ice-cap missed the ship which was to have picked them up, the expedition was a great success. Even their enforced stay through the winter was put to good use. Nansen studied the techniques developed by the Eskimos and learned many useful skills, besides gathering material for a book on Eskimo life which was published in 1891.

Even though by the age of twenty-eight Nansen was one of the first men to cross Greenland and had become an international hero, his next expedition was to dwarf all this. He was first inspired with the idea of his voyage after reading a newspaper article written by Professor Henrik Mohn in 1884. It was about the discovery of some wreckage from a ship, the *Jeanette*, found embedded in an ice-floe. Apparently, over a period of three years, the wreckage had travelled a considerable distance on a north–south axis. His plan was founded on this information and on Nansen's own knowledge of the kinds of driftwood and microscopic algae found on the east coast of Greenland and in the Chukchi Sea. Quite simply, he wanted to use the currents and winds which were

moving such things to carry him across the North Pole.

In 1891 Nansen presented his idea to the Royal Geographical Society of Christiania. His main theme was, "if a floe could drift right across the unknown region, that drift might be enlisted in the service of exploration." Nansen reasoned that taking into account the effect of the wind on the current, there should be a resulting westerly current in the Arctic ice pack which passed across the Pole towards the Greenland area. Previously, explorers had sailed up to the great Arctic ice barrier, disembarked, and aimed for the Pole on foot, being rightly afraid of their boat becoming ice-bound or crushed. Nansen wished to have a special ship made, and then deliberately become ice-bound off eastern Siberia. He would continue towards the Pole on the slow but inevitable current which swept through the ice. He knew that the current would not necessarily take him exactly across the Pole, but, as he said, "Our object is to investigate the great unknown regions that surround the Pole."

Once Nansen had collected enough evidence to show that the ice of the Polar Sea drifted from Siberia towards Spitzbergen, it only remained for him to build a boat which would be lifted and not crushed as the ice closed in. Following Nansen's directions, the Norwegian engineer Colin Archer drew up the plans. The ship, the *Fram* (Norwegian for "Forward"), began to take shape. This choice of name for the ship was very characteristic of Nansen. He believed that the secret of his success was to burn his bridges behind him. "Then there is no choice for you but forward."

The *Fram* was not very beautiful to look at since she had been designed both for strength and to slip above the ice blocks as they pressed inwards. The *Fram*'s width, 36 feet, was almost one third of her length (keel: 102 feet), and with her rounded smooth sides she looked and was, blunt, sturdy and strongly built.

Carefully packed with enough rations to last five years, and with a mass of scientific equipment on board, the *Fram* and her thirteen man crew sailed on 24 June 1893, nine years after Nansen had read Professor Mohn's article. Amongst the crew were Otto Neumann Sverdrup, the first officer, who had been with Nansen on the Greenland expedition, and Lieutenant Hofalmar Johansen who had signed on as a stoker. There was also a doctor, a harpooner, a watchmaker, and an electrician.

Pausing for a few days at Khabarova to take on thirty-four dogs for sledge-pulling, and for certain repairs, the *Fram* continued through the Kara Sea and the Chelyuskin Strait until it reached the ice-barrier at 77°44′N. On 20 September. They moved the ship to a large ice-block. A few days passed as the ice gradually closed in and bound the *Fram*.

The temperature was −8·5°C as the *Fram* began its long drift among the five million square miles of misty polar ice. Any faults in her design would soon become very obvious. But, as the ice pressure built up against the sides of the ship, the design proved itself: the ship rose up as the ice slid beneath. Relieved, the crew could turn to their scientific work. Magnetic and meteorological measurements, surveying, depth and current testing, the health of the crew, all these and much else had to be investigated and observed. Since the rudder had been removed and the engine dismantled and stored, the windmill which had been brought to power the dynamo had to be continually re-aligned with the wind.

As the months passed it became clear to Nansen that there was one problem which was going to make him increasingly restless. In spite of all the various experiments and activities, the actual rate of the drift was very slow.

During the second winter on the ice pack, Nansen announced his determination to leave the ship and try to reach the Pole by foot, kayak and sledge. After waiting for the weather to improve, he left the ship on 14 March 1895, choosing Lieutenant Johansen to travel with him and leaving Captain Sverdrup in command. They took with them two kayaks, three sledges, twenty-seven dogs, guns, double reindeer-skin sleeping bags, various scientific instruments, and a supply of dried fish and meat. Their equipment weighed about 1460 pounds all together. Once again, Nansen was burning his bridges behind him. It would be impossible to find the drifting *Fram* on their return. They had no choice therefore but to reach Spitzbergen or Franz Josef Land on their own. Then, they hoped, they would be picked up by a whaling boat that would take them back to Norway. So began their incredible journey. It was to be fifteen months from the time they left the *Fram* until their eventual meeting with the English explorer Jackson on Franz Josef Land on 17 June 1896.

By 15 November 1895 the *Fram* had reached its most northerly point in the whole journey, 85° 58′ north latitude, 66° 31′ east longitude. The record has been unrivalled by any other boat, with the exception of modern submarines. Meanwhile, Nansen was hoping that by travelling as lightly and quickly as possible, he and Johansen would reach the Pole before the Arctic winter closed in again. By April, however, Nansen was beginning to doubt if it was advisable to continue north for much longer. Temperatures were already down to 47 c below zero, and the increasingly difficult ice was steadily exhausting them. By 8 April they finally admitted that the vast jungle of ice was impossible to penetrate. They hoisted the Norwegian flag at what was then the most northerly point reached by man, less than 250 miles from the Pole. Wearily they began their southward retreat towards Franz Josef Land.

Supplies soon began to run short, and they had to kill off some of their loyal dogs

to feed the other sledge-pullers. At this point Nansen made one of his most serious mistakes. He forgot to wind their chronometers one morning, and it became impossible for them to work out their longitude accurately. Supplies became so reduced that only the chance appearance of a seal or bear which they managed to shoot and eat, saved their lives.

Almost exhausted, they set up a camp from August to May—unaware that the Jackson-Harmsworth expedition had a firmly established base only ninety-four miles away. They managed to last out, mainly on a diet of bear and walrus. They used the blubber as fuel in spite of its soot and grease. Finally, on 17 June, Nansen happened to meet a member of the Jackson-Harmsworth expedition on Cape Flood. On 26 July, when fresh provisions were shipped in for Jackson's expedition by the *Windward*, Nansen and Johansen were able to leave for home and safety.

By 13 August 1896, the *Fram* had reached a place just north of Spitzbergen but it was still necessary to use dynamite to break the grip of the ice round the vessel. On the same day Jackson brought Nansen and Johansen back to Vardo in Norway. By 27 August, the whole crew of the *Fram* were reunited with Nansen and Johansen at Tromo and on 9 September, the expedition finally travelled back to a triumphant reception in Christiania.

Although the expedition had not actually reached the Pole, they had not lost a single man throughout their long exposure to the Arctic conditions—a rare achievement. They had also brought back a wealth of scientific information about a little-known part of the world, for example, the nature of the currents in the Arctic ocean and its surprisingly great depth in some places. Last but not least, the design of the *Fram* had been so good that Amundsen borrowed it from Nansen for his journey to the South Pole some years later.

East of the Sun and west of the Moon

Once there was a Prince who was young and handsome. He lived alone in a marvellous palace surrounded by a garden full of trees, shrubs and flowers. He had numerous servants and a wise old tutor, all of whom were men, and he did not even know that there were women in the world. His parents had protected him all his life from learning of the existence of women, for it had been predicted when he was born that at the age of twenty he would be in danger of losing his life for love's sake.

So he lived with little gentleness or tenderness around him. His greatest pleasure was his garden and he spent many nights awake on his balcony watching the flowers peacefully sleep. One night as he stood there he saw three beautiful swans land at the top of a tall tree. He watched closely, thrilled by the thought of such lovely birds inhabiting the garden. But despite his care, he lost sight of the swans and instead saw three glorious creatures descending among the branches. They looked very like men, but they were lighter, more graceful, somehow different in shape.

"What are they?" the Prince asked himself. Desiring a closer look, he ran down the stairs and out into the garden, but they had passed out of sight. Reaching the tree where the swans had landed, he climbed to the top; and there he found three swan skins, which the creatures had discarded.

"One of these I will keep," he said to himself, and he took the fairest, brought it back to the palace and locked it in a secret com-partment in a trunk in his bedchamber. Then he stood again on the balcony, watching the tall tree.

After a while, the creatures returned to the tree, climbed up and looked for their swan skins. When they found one skin missing, they searched for a long time. At last, two flew away, and one remained.

The Prince descended from his balcony and went to the tree. He saw the creature that was not unlike a man wringing its hands in distress.

"What are you?" he asked. The creature raised a tear-stained face.

"A maiden in despair. I must have my swan skin. Do you have it?"

"Not I," said the Prince. "I have burned it." For he did not want to let this strange being depart. "But what do you mean, a 'maiden'? What is that?"

"Why a woman, and a Princess. I am one of the Cloud King's daughters. But of course you are making fun of me, now," she said.

"Indeed," cried the Prince, "I am not. I have never met a woman before. I did not know such beings as you existed."

"Have you no mother?" she asked, bewildered.

"What is that?" said the Prince intently.

At this the Princess felt such pity for the poor young man that she forgot her own misfortune. She sat down on the grass and explained to him as best she could about women and men, love and marriage, mothers, fathers and children. The Prince listened eagerly and when she had finished he sent servants to his father, requesting him to visit the palace, and announcing (for he had decided this quite of his own accord) that he was getting married.

The following day, the King and Queen arrived. They were enchanted by the Princess, but disturbed to see that she did not really want to marry their son. They feared that she would bring him the heartbreak that had been predicted for him.

"My father would not want me to marry a mortal," the Princess repeated. But she could not return home without her swan shape, for her father's palace was East of the Sun and West of the Moon, and she had no way of getting there. So the Prince and the Princess were married; the King and Queen gave up their thrones and presented them with the kingdom to rule over.

At first they were very happy. The young Queen appeared to decide that her place was with her husband and that she must forget her home. Yet secretly she longed to return and by devious means she discovered where her swan shape was hidden. One morning the young King awoke to find that the window was open, and his beautiful bride was gone.

He decided to take his own life, and, summoning his tutor, he declared his intentions.

"Your Majesty must not do this," cried the old man. "Trust yourself to me. We will find your Queen."

"She is East of the Sun and West of the Moon," said the young King sadly. "We cannot go there."

"Please trust me," said the tutor. "If we begin our journey in good faith, we will reach her."

They prepared themselves for a long journey, but although they had many maps and the advice of the most experienced travellers in the kingdom, they did not know which way to go. They set off through the forests that bordered the kingdom and wandered for many days and nights. Occa-

sionally they met a beggar or a solitary woodsman.

"Do you know the way to the city East of the Sun and West of the Moon?" the tutor would ask. And the person would reply, "There is an old man (or an old woman or a wild man) two days (or two weeks or two years) from here. I think he knows."

Then the King and his tutor would thank the speaker and continue on, obeying every instruction, following every direction, but all in vain.

At last they met a fierce dwarf, with a long, hooked nose and upturned eyes, whose matted beard touched the ground. The tutor asked his weary question.

"Can you, dear Sir, in your wisdom and knowledge of this world, direct us to the city East of the Sun and West of the Moon? For this young King is married to one of the Cloud King's daughters and she is at her father's palace. We have travelled so long he is losing his faith and daily he broods upon death. I beseech your assistance."

The dwarf snorted fiercely. "I must have time to think. Meet me tomorrow in the same place." He stalked away.

"He will not help us," sighed the King.

"I think he will," the tutor said. They waited all night and until the afternoon. Finally the dwarf returned, holding a long pipe.

"I can only do the best I can," he said angrily, and he lay on the ground and blew into his pipe, making a hideous noise. All at once the air was loud with bird-cries. Birds of many sizes and colours hovered in the air. Some landed near the dwarf's feet, while a little owl perched in the middle of his beard.

"Have you been to the city East of the Sun and West of the Moon?" boomed the Dwarf.

The birds shook their heads. "No," they chorused. "Not even the eagle has been there. It is far too far."

"That's enough, then," the Dwarf thundered. "You may go." He waved his hands and the birds flew upwards with a great rush and disappeared.

"We will try again," he said, blowing a terrible blast on his pipe. The sound echoed and grew until the forest was filled with whistlings and groanings and four vague, cold shapes blew around overhead. The King and his tutor shivered. The Dwarf, almost black in the face from his effort, addressed the strange shapes. "You winds, North, South, East and West, I need your assistance. Can you blow this young King to the Cloud King's palace?"

The winds chattered together. "Not East of the Sun and West of the Moon," they replied. "It is far too far. Try our brothers, the side-winds. They may be able to help you." And the four winds swirled around for a moment, and then disappeared.

The Dwarf lay down again. "I can only do my best," he said, scowling; and contorting his face in a dreadful way, he blew as if he would burst his lungs. The forest swayed back and forth and a wild howling filled the air. Three other shapes tossed overhead.

"North-East, North-West, South-West winds, can you carry this young man to the Cloud King's palace," asked the Dwarf.

They tossed and moaned. "Ask our brother, South-East. He is the strongest."

Suddenly a great shriek was heard and the air became bitterly cold. The South-East wind roared into view.

"Why do you call me, Miserable One?" he howled in fury.

The Dwarf became very polite. "Oh great and gracious wind," he began, "this young King is wed to one of the Cloud Princesses—"

"Aha," cried the wind, "you are the one she weeps for. I have seen her just now. Come with me. I will take you to her."

"Wait," said the Dwarf. "Fetch the Cloud King's chariot, that he may ride in safety."

"Very well," said the wind; and sucking in an enormous amount of air until he looked like a formless puffy cloud, he suddenly went "Whoosh!" and shot away out of sight. Within minutes he was back again, pulling the Cloud King's golden chariot.

Gravely the young King said farewell to his tutor and stepped into the chariot to travel where no mortal man had ever been. The South-East wind blew so hard that he outdistanced the birds and the fastest clouds. The young King, looking down, saw great trees flattened by the blast of their passage. Then they lifted away from the earth and for a few moments he could see only layers of cloud until, shining brightly, he saw the gilded towers of the city East of the Sun and West of the Moon.

As they came closer, the young King saw his bride sitting over a pile of dirty clothes, and weeping as if her heart would break.

"If only I had not left him," she sighed. "I did love him so." Just then she raised her head and saw her husband before her. "Are you real? How did you come?" she cried.

"The South-East wind brought me," he said, holding her close. "But, tell me, why do you bother with this pile of clothes?"

"It is my punishment for marrying a mortal. My father has made me my sisters' slave. But now he will change his mind. No other mortal man has ever come here, and he must realize how different you are."

True enough, when the Cloud King saw that his daughter's husband had made the impossible journey he was so impressed that he gave the young couple his blessing. He even consented to his daughter's returning to earth.

After several days of feasting, the South-East wind, who had been resting all this time, announced that he had business elsewhere. So the young King and Queen climbed into the chariot, left the city East of the Sun and West of the Moon, and were blown back to earth. There they were received with great joy, and they ruled happily over their kingdom for many years.

The conquest of Everest

When George Everest, surveyor-general of India, first discovered and measured the highest mountain in the world in 1856, he must have had little idea that almost a century would pass before anyone climbed to its summit. The peak, five and a half miles high, was known to the local Tibetans as *Chomolunga*, "Mother Goddess of the Land". It was so high that it was difficult even to measure it accurately in the rarefied air. Although some mountaineers argued that there might be more difficult climbs, like nearby Kangchen Junga (28,168 feet), the fascination of Everest as the highest peak remained. Apart from reconnaissance expeditions, the successful expedition sponsored by the Alpine Club of the Royal Geographical Society in 1953, was the eighth team in thirty years to attempt the climb.

Just how dangerous Everest could be was in no doubt since two explorers (Mallory and Irvine) had vanished without trace in 1924 while climbing in a mist.

The kinds of problems which very high mountains present to the climbers are in some ways like the worst aspects of space and arctic travel combined but without their considerable reliance on technology. Not only is the high altitude environment

totally hostile to human or other life, but the climbers must carry everything they need with them: oxygen, ice-axes, ropes, crampons, food and fuel. Unlike space and arctic explorers, mountaineers have no command module or permanent base to retreat into but must use tents and sleeping bags where there is enough flat space to do so.

Relying on their experience and skills, mountaineers realize that apart from the technicalities of climbing, the better they are at surviving ceaseless cold, wind, ice and snow, the better will be their chances of reaching the summit. As if these were not enough to contend with, the mountain itself is continually changing, as masses of ice and snow break away and re-form. On the lower part of Everest there is a two mile long, 2000-foot high ice-fall, a vast mass of ice always moving and changing, with some blocks as big as houses. Aluminium ladders which bolt together are carried up and used to cross the bigger crevasses which open up in the ice. Only then can the route be made safer by ice-chopping and ropes so that the Sherpa porters can carry up the supplies to pitch the next camp.

In order to advance up the mountain it was necessary to have a whole series of camps reaching up to the summit. All this was to establish two climbers at the highest camp with enough food, oxygen and energy left to make the last and hardest climb to the top. Afterwards, of course, there still remained the problem of getting back.

It would be difficult to find two men less alike than the two climbers who finally reached the summit: Sir Edmund Hillary and Tenzing Norgay. Hillary was a tall, athletic, New Zealander, born in Auckland in 1919. By profession he was a bee-keeper but mountains and exploring had been his ruling passions ever since he saw his first mountain when he was sixteen, on a school ski-ing party to the New Zealand volcano Ruapehu. Hillary learned not only from actually climbing mountains in New Zea-

land but also from the people he climbed with. In particular he learned from Harry Ayres, a leading climber who was very skilled at snow and ice climbing.

Tenzing, on the other hand, was a smaller and slightly older man whose toughness earned him the nickname "Tiger". He was born in the Himalayas, in the Sherpa district south of Everest called Solo Khumbu. Very experienced and used to high altitudes, Tenzing made his living carrying loads in the mountains. He was Sirdar (chief porter) on several expeditions before 1953, notably on two Swiss attempts. In fact the Sherpa hillmen formed a vital part of every Himalayan expedition. Without their help all the supplies needed could not be carried. As Hillary said afterwards, it took "eleven weeks of severe toil and the labours of two hundred men to place two climbers within reach of the unclimbed summit."

To organize and lead the whole expedition, a man of special talents was obviously required. Colonel John Hunt was eventually chosen. He soon made a good impression on Hillary by announcing his intention of "leading from the front". He was as good as his word and carried loads up to 27,000 feet himself to support the summit climbers. His planning was always very thorough and he believed in participating actively at every stage and in every job. Like Hillary, Hunt had discovered mountains early in his youth and had climbed in many parts of the world. He also brought with him the experience gained from training troops in mountain warfare.

Not only did the expedition combine the skills its members had gained on other mountains besides Everest (which Tenzing had already climbed to 28,000 feet); there were also the previous unsuccessful expeditions from which to learn. Among these was the brilliant Swiss attempt in 1952. The Swiss had pioneered the new idea of approaching the mountain from the south, which involved crossing the 2000-foot ice-fall. Hillary and Shipton had seen the route taken from the neighbouring Pumori ridge and believed it to be the best way up. The British expedition was also able to use the supplies of oxygen and tinned food left behind by the Swiss.

According to Tenzing's account of the 1952 expedition, they could have actually reached the summit but, because of exhaustion and worsening weather, they would have been unable to make the descent. One stage of 650 feet up to 28,000 feet, had taken five hours of incredible effort to climb and still another 1000 feet remained. Both Tenzing and Lambert had realized that to go on would have meant death, so they stopped and turned back. They remembered how others, like Mallory and Irvine, had disappeared for ever, at the same height but on the other side of the mountain.

The weather helped to produce a different story the next year when Hillary and Tenzing set off from camp IX on 29 May at 6.30 a.m. Although the temperature had sunk to $-27°c$ in the night, and Hillary had to cook his boots to unfreeze them, the weather was good, for Everest. Dressing essentially consisted of putting on boots. They already had on six layers of clothing and three different layers of gloves: silk, wool and windproof. Rubbing cream on their faces against the burning wind and sun and pulling on snow-goggles against the glare, they set off.

The air was so thin that Hillary felt his thirty-pound load crushing him to the ground until he turned on the oxygen and breathed deeply. Outside the tent they were immediately faced with very steep slopes covered with deep powdery snow still lying in the shadow and very cold. They climbed out straight away over the vast southern face of the mountain with a drop of thousands of feet of rocks and snow below them. Eventually they reached the summit ridge, not rising too steeply but still sharp and narrow. Immediately they ran into a serious hazard.

The wind crust formed on the surface of the snow was just too weak to support their weight, so that they sank through up to the knee with every step. Staying on the safer left-hand side of the ridge they struggled up gasping for breath, at the same time keeping a precarious balance against the wind until they came to firmer snow.

Fortunately, the next surprise was a pleasant one, two oxygen bottles, nearly covered with snow, left by Evans and Bourdillon, the other summit team. Both bottles were one-third full, which meant that the oxygen they were already carrying only had to get them to the summit and back, instead of all the way down to camp IX. Hillary calculated that this gave them an extra hour. With this comfort behind them they were confronted with the final 400 feet of snow face leading up to the summit itself. Looking back, Hillary describes how the final ridge seemed never-ending. After two hours of chipping out steps he was wondering how long they could keep it up when he suddenly realized that he had reached "the last bump . . . Almost ahead of me the ridge dropped steeply away . . . out in the distance I could see the pastel shades and fleecy clouds of the highlands of Tibet." A "few more whacks" with the ice axe, and they stood on the summit. Hillary remembers his own astonishment and relief, and Tenzing's delight, as they shook hands and congratulated each other. They had enough time for Hillary to take photographs "in every direction", and for Tenzing (as a devout Buddhist) to bury some food as an offering to the Gods of Chomolunga. Hillary agreed that Everest had been kind to them at the end.

After a safe return, the news of Hillary and Tenzing's triumph spread rapidly. In London it coincided with the eve of the coronation of Queen Elizabeth II, so among the many honours they received were a Knighthood for Hillary and Colonel Hunt and the George Medal for Tenzing.

Six miles under the sea

Men and women have made journeys to almost every corner of the earth. They have climbed mountains, crossed deserts and explored dangerous rivers. They have even ventured beyond our planet into space. But there is still one vast region about which we know very little: the oceans.

With an average depth of about two and a half miles, there is far more sea than land on Earth. The bottom of the sea is as varied as the surface of the land, too. There are mountains almost as high as Mount Everest and canyons as deep as the Colorado Grand Canyon. Some seas, like the North Sea are only about 400 feet deep, while the very deepest part of all, a trench in the Pacific Ocean is 37,800 feet deep—almost seven miles.

It is no wonder that from ancient times we have been fascinated by the possibilities of exploring the sea bed. A journey to the bottom of the sea, however, is no easy journey. First there is the problem of breathing; then there is the great weight of millions of tons of water to be withstood. And in the darkness, where the sun never reaches, who knows what strange creatures may be lurking.

Even in ancient times men caught fish in the sea and travelled for short voyages in simple boats. In warm countries, where the sea was shallow, clear and warm close to the shore, men would dive to catch shell fish. Pearls especially have been found in this way for thousands of years. However, these early divers had no efficient diving equipment and could only stay under water for as long as they could hold their breath. The Assyrians were skilled divers nearly 3000 years ago and were able to stay under water for longer by carrying extra supplies of air in animal skins. By Roman times, a simple diving suit had been invented with a mask to cover the diver's face and a leather pipe going up to the surface to provide air —rather like a snorkel.

One of the first people to explore the sea scientifically was Charles Wyville Thomson, a marine scientist. During the 1860s, using the latest diving suits, he went down 600 fathoms (1 fathom = 6 feet) and discovered that a great variety of plants and animals lived there. In 1872 he sailed on board H.M.S. *Challenger*, a ship especially equipped for scientific undersea discovery. The *Challenger* left England on 21 December and by February was in the Antarctic. Thomson led a team of scientists whose mission was to find out about the depths of the oceans and to examine the types of life that were to be found there. On board ship were chemical and biological laboratories where the scientists could examine sea plants under microscopes and carry out their experiments.

During 1874 and 1875 they voyaged about the China Seas and found a part of the sea which was 4574 fathoms, then the greatest depth ever recorded. Whenever he could, Professor Thomson started up scientific observation stations so that a continuous watch could be kept on the oceans. He organized dredgings to collect samples of life and made a special study of deep sea currents. When the *Challenger* arrived back at Spithead on 24 May 1876, Thomson and his team had collected plant, animal and mineral specimens from depths of over 3000 fathoms.

The *Challenger's* pioneer voyage inspired undersea explorers throughout the rest of the nineteenth century and into the twentieth. As equipment became more sophisticated, divers became more adventurous. In 1934 Dr William Beebe and Otis Barton went down in a new type of diving craft called a bathysphere. This was a steel ball which could be lowered on a cable from a boat on the surface. Beebe and Barton descended over 3000 feet in their bathysphere. Although it enabled them to go deeper, they were always in danger because of the risk of the cable breaking.

August Piccard, the Swiss scientist, was interested in both balloon flight and underwater exploration. He designed a bathyscaphe. This worked rather like a balloon under the sea.

It carried iron ballast to make it sink. When the diver wanted to return to the surface, the ballast was shot out and the lightened craft floated upwards. In 1948 Piccard went down 750 fathoms off the African coast near Dakar and five years later, in a new bathyscaphe, he and his son descended 1732 fathoms. Unlike Beebe and Barton's bathysphere, Piccard's bathyscaphe did not need a cable to connect it with a surface ship. It could travel up and down under its own power and was so successful that the U.S. navy bought it in 1959.

That same year a special journey of exploration was planned, to the deepest part of the ocean, at Challenger Deep near the Island of Guam in the Pacific Ocean. The dive was to be made in a new bathyscaphe called the *Trieste*, by Jacques Piccard and an American Marines officer called Donald Walsh. They made a number of trial dives before attempting Challenger Deep. After one of them it was found that the great pressure of the sea had almost broken the craft into three parts, and urgent strengthening and repairs had to be made.

At last, on 23 January 1960, everything was ready and Piccard and Walsh went aboard. Slowly the *Trieste* went down, passing first through sunlit waters, then through shadow. By the time they were at a depth of 200 fathoms the light was very dim and they turned on the *Trieste's* powerful searchlights. Beyond their beams, the ocean was completely dark except for the occasional lights of the strange fish that live at these great depths. The *Trieste* continued to descend until it had reached the world record depth of 35,784 feet.

Everyone was delighted with the achievement of Piccard and Walsh and with the efficient way the *Trieste* had performed even at the bottom of the deepest ocean. That same year more dives were made in the *Trieste* and then it was taken away to the workshops to be repaired and improved. A special mechanical arm was fixed to the undersea craft. This arm was operated by remote control and could be used to pick things up from the bed of the sea.

Piccard's bathyscaphe was a wonderful invention for exploring the bottom of the deepest oceans. Jacques Yves Cousteau was more interested in exploring the shallower parts of the sea. Cousteau, a French naval officer and Emile Gagnon, a French engineer, invented a new type of diving apparatus called an aqualung. This consisted of cylinders of compressed air which were fixed to the diver's back and enabled him to swim about under water for long periods. Cousteau had long experience of goggle diving and fishing, especially in the Mediterranean Sea, where he had founded the Research Undersea Rescue Group for the French Navy. He was often in action under the sea off the coast of Africa and in the Red Sea and his beautiful photographs of undersea life and scenes have become world famous.

After the Second World War Cousteau bought an old mine-sweeper called the *Calypso* and refitted it as a scientific ship for undersea exploration. On board was a Galeazzi Tower, a special container which carried a crew and could be lowered 1000 feet into the sea. Cousteau's crew of underwater explorers also had diving saucers, small craft driven by water-jet engines which could move about at the bottom of the sea and underwater scooters driven by electric engines. An observation compartment was built under the *Calypso* so that scientists could look through eight portholes and watch the fish swimming by.

In 1951 Cousteau led a team of twenty-one scientists in the *Calypso* on a voyage of exploration under the Red Sea. Sharks always made their work risky and one day when Cousteau and his friend Pierre Drach were exploring in their aqualungs, a shark approached them. At that moment Drach was busy examining some samples of tiny undersea life and did not seem aware of the shark. Cousteau, however, realized the danger at once and made frantic efforts to warn his friend. While Drach carried on with his work the shark was all the time swimming around them and could have attacked at any moment. Fortunately it turned and swam away, leaving Cousteau and Drach to continue their exploration.

Cousteau and his team of divers made many exciting discoveries, including a cargo of ancient Roman pots from a merchant ship which had sunk about 2000 years before. In 1962 Cousteau and his friends built a special cylinder-shaped undersea house which they sent to the bottom of the sea off the coast of southern France. This unusual home had beds, an electric cooker, a telephone and other home comforts. Albert Falco and Claude Wesly lived in this house for a week. During this time they went out to explore under the sea and then returned to their home through a special opening. At the end of the week they returned to the surface.

Since that time underwater exploration has continued. In 1969 the first international conference to discuss the wealth of the oceans was held at Brighton. This conference was called Oceanology International and while it was going on a phone message was received from an American crew working at the bottom of the Pacific Ocean in a sea laboratory where they were to stay for ninety days.

Great advances had been made during the 1960s in the building of craft for underwater exploration. The Americans had a strange egg-shaped craft called *Deepstar* which had a crew of two men and could reach depths of 4000 feet. *Deepstar* has cameras and searchlights which can be operated from the two forward portholes and the crew keep in touch with a ship on the surface by telephone. It is driven by battery-powered electric motors and has a remote-controlled mechanical arm which picks things up from the sea bed and drops them into a retractable basket.

In Britain a remarkable sea exploration craft called *Bacchus* has been built in which as many as six men will be able to live and work at the bottom of the sea. British scientists have also been working on an undersea vehicle which moves along the sea bed on spiked wheels.

The dangers and difficulties of exploring the bottom of the sea and discovering the mysteries of the oceans may be even greater than exploring space but the rewards are probably greater. The sea bed contains oil and natural gas which is already being used and it is possible that in the future underwater farming will provide us with much needed extra food supplies. Ocean Research Equipment, an American company, have discovered gold at the bottom of the Pacific Ocean. With so much to be gained and so much that is wonderful to discover, it can be no surprise that there is a growing interest in exploration under the sea.

Man on the Moon

It was 10.56 in the morning, but the sky was black. The scene was utterly desolate, the ground covered in dust—black dust which nonetheless reflected the dazzling, unclouded rays of the sun. In front, as far as the narrow curved horizon, rocks and craters cast inky shadows. Just two people were there: two men who had completed the longest, most historic journey ever made. One of the two stood poised to take the most historic step ever taken.

This moment was in the morning of 22 July 1969. The two men, named Neil Armstrong and Edwin Aldrin, were about to step out onto the Moon. The vessel which had brought them from their own planet seemed tiny, frail and vulnerable compared with the utter desolation on all sides. Even so there could be no greater contrast than the one between *Eagle*, the Lunar Module of the Apollo 11 spacecraft, and the crude frail wooden sailing ships of the early explorers on Earth.

Perhaps it was both logical and fitting that the greatest of all man's journeys should have been made by Americans. For America had been the "new-found-land" that had fired men's imaginations for so long in the sixteenth and seventeenth centuries. And America itself had seen countless journeys of adventure and discovery as the early pioneers and settlers explored its apparently limitless expanse. Not least, for two hundred years America had been a symbol of hope for a better life for millions of people from all over the world who had been drawn to it. Now another, stranger new world was in sight.

Out of sight of Armstrong and Aldrin, in orbit around the Moon, was the mission's "mother ship" the Command Module *Columbia*, with Michael Collins, the third Apollo 11 astronaut in control.

The journey had begun six days before, 240,000 miles away across the empty vacuum of space, when all three had blasted off from Cape Kennedy, Florida, carried by a giant three-stage Saturn rocket. Command and Landing modules had been joined together then, as Apollo accelerated to 24,500 m.p.h. and burst free of Earth's gravity on a course for the Moon.

Then, after three days' travel, at 1.22 p.m. on 19 July, they had begun to make preparations for separating the two modules and entering orbit around the Moon, both essential preliminaries to the actual descent and landing.

Apollo's rocket motor was fired twice, first to put the spacecraft into an elliptical orbit 70 to 196 miles above the lunar surface; then, when that had been safely accomplished, to edge it closer, 62 to 76 miles up. At last, Armstrong and Aldrin said farewell to Collins and crawled through the narrow tube connecting the larger three-man Command Module *Columbia* to the much smaller Landing Module *Eagle*. Then came separation, and *Eagle*'s electronic guidance and control systems began the delicate job of bringing the Landing Module down in the pre-selected target area. This lay in the "Sea of Tranquillity", chosen because it seemed smooth and free from large rocks and craters.

The astronauts' lives depended on a smooth landing. If *Eagle* came to rest at an angle greater than 12 degrees she could never take off again. The Sea of Tranquillity was first discovered by an astronomer in the sixteenth century and had been scoured by hundreds of telescopes ever since—in particular by the men of the American space research centre before they programmed *Eagle*'s computers. Surely nothing could go wrong.

But in spite of all the research that had been carried out, the closer *Eagle* drew to the landing site the less Aldrin, at the controls, liked the look of it. Instead of a smooth surface there were enormous rocks, and deep, wide craters . . .

Aldrin took over manual control from the computers. Eye and hand replaced electronics as he "flew" *Eagle* four miles beyond the original landing site before gently easing her down. Gently . . . feeling his way as the dust clouds raised by the descent rockets billowed up. Gently again until the 68-inch tripod undercarriage touched solid ground and the warning light flashed in the cabin.

"Cabin light on . . . engine off . . . the *Eagle* has landed," radioed Armstrong;

The first triumph was achieved! Men had reached the Moon—*Eagle* was resting safely, at an angle of only 4 degrees. All around her stretched the most alien environment any explorer had ever landed on. A place where there had been no life of any kind since time began.

Armstrong and Aldrin now had six and a half hours of rest to prepare for the greatest moment of all, when they would leave the comparative safety of *Eagle* and step out onto the Moon's surface.

They were further from help and home by distance, but also less alone, than any explorers before them had ever been. From blast-off to Moonlanding they had been in continual radio and television communication with their colleagues in the U.S. space programme. They had been watched and listened to by hundreds of millions of people all over the world. At the moment when Neil Armstrong opened the hatch of *Eagle* and took the first cautious steps down the descent ladder, it is estimated that 600,000,000 people on Earth were watching. . . .

Slowly, in gravity one-sixth that of Earth, clothed in a space suit and life support pack, Armstrong climbed down eight of the ladder's nine rungs. On the ninth, he paused a long moment. "I'm going off the L.M. now," he radioed to Earth's millions. "That's one small step for a man, one giant leap for mankind."

And so he dropped lightly to the gritty surface below. There was much work to do. Rocks and moondust were collected, scientific instruments set up. Then, 18 minutes afterwards, his commander, Edwin (Buzz) Aldrin joined him on the ground. Together they planted a small American flag, set up more experiments, collected more rock samples. The minutes passed quickly; just two and a half hours after he had left *Eagle,* Armstrong was back inside. Aldrin had returned half an hour earlier.

The second great triumph had been achieved; the second period of greatest danger safely negotiated. But at once there were fresh problems to overcome, and the worst dangers of all: the return journey. On the outward trip, at any point until the final descent and touch-down, the astronauts could have changed their minds, abandoned the mission or gone back if something had gone wrong. But from touch-down onwards there were no second chances. Lift-off from the Moon, the rendezvous in space with the orbiting *Columbia*, the final re-separation of the two modules and abandonment of *Eagle*, all these problems had to go perfectly if fuel and oxygen supplies were to last and

the three men reach Earth again alive!

Many things were left behind on the Moon's surface: the scientific devices Armstrong and Aldrin had set up, the flag, the special overshoes they had worn to help them walk on the soft moondust, the whole descent stage of the L.M. itself—abandoned now that its job had been done, serving at last as a launching platform for *Eagle*'s blast-off. Left behind also was a television camera, focused on *Eagle*. . . .

No-one of the hundreds of millions who watched, 240,000 miles away on Earth will ever forget the feeling as they waited for *Eagle*'s rockets to ignite, listening to the countdown, perhaps feeling as if they, like the television cameras, were being abandoned in the sunscorched desolation of the Sea of Tranquillity.

"5–4–3–2–1–*Zero*. Ignition . . . lift-off!" *Eagle* leaped into the dark lunar sky, and the return journey had begun.

Armstrong and Aldrin had spent in all just 21 hours and 37 minutes on the Moon. They had claimed no territory, nor sought either conquest or profit. Yet their journey was the culmination of every expedition of discovery ever made since men first began to wander the Earth.

Behind them they left things which connected them with those earlier journeys, successful and unsuccessful, and with all the brave, foolhardy or ambitious men who had ever made them. Their flag. The insignia and medals of five astronauts (three American and two Russian) who had died in the course of their countries' space research programmes. Tiny silicone discs bearing messages of peace and goodwill from the world's leaders. Most important of all, perhaps, they left a small plaque with these words: "Here men from the planet Earth first set foot upon the Moon. July 1969 A.D. We came in peace for all mankind."

The plaque was signed by astronauts Armstrong, Aldrin and Collins, and by President Nixon of the United States.